EXCEL

From Beginners to Pro| Simplify your Work and Dominate Data with Smart Excel Strategies. Secret winning Formulas with Step-by-Step Tutorials to Stand Out from the Crowd

Study Solution For Success

© Copyright 2023 - All rights reserved.

The content contained within this book may not be reproduced, duplicated or transmitted without direct written permission from the author or the publisher.

Under no circumstances will any blame or legal responsibility be held against the publisher, or author, for any damages, reparation, or monetary loss due to the information contained within this book. Either directly or indirectly.

Legal Notice:

This book is copyright protected. This book is only for personal use. You cannot amend, distribute, sell, use, quote or paraphrase any part, or the content within this book, without the consent of the author or publisher.

Disclaimer Notice:

Please note the information contained within this document is for educational and entertainment purposes only. All effort has been executed to present accurate, up to date, and reliable, complete information. No warranties of any kind are declared or implied. Readers acknowledge that the author is not engaging in the rendering of legal, financial, medical or professional advice. The content within this book has been derived from various sources. Please consult a licensed professional before attempting any techniques outlined in this book.

By reading this document, the reader agrees that under no circumstances is the author responsible for any losses, direct or indirect, which are incurred as a result of the use of information contained within this document, including, but not limited to, — errors, omissions, or inaccuracies.

TABLE OF CONTENTS

INTRODUCTION — 6
- Excel Tools 6
- File Formats That Are Supported in Excel 6
- Terminologies of Excel 7
- MS Excel Shortcut Keys 11

CHAPTER 1: Excel Cases (Formatting Rows and Columns) — 21
- Entering, Editing, and Managing Data 21
- Hint and Tips 23
- Formatting Cells 39

CHAPTER 2: Basic Formulas and Functions and Making Calculations in Excel — 54
- How You Should Enter Formulas in Excel 54
- Creating a Simple Formula Example in Excel 54
- Creating the Formulas that Refer to the Other Cell inside the Same Worksheet 55
- Create a Formula that Links to the Other Workbooks 56
- Use of Apostrophes for Enclosing and to Full the File Name and the Worksheet Name 57
- Basic Formulas and Functions for Excel Workflow 58

CHAPTER 3: How to Create Charts and Graphs in Excel — 64
- Graphs and Charts in Excel 64
- Forms and Types of Charts 64
- Best Ways to Create a Chart and Graph 68
- How to Make Chart Data in Excel 68
- How to Make a Chart in Excel 69
- How to Make a Graph in Excel 87

CHAPTER 4: Data Importation (CSV, Text File) — 89

Data Importation from Different Sources in Workbook 89

CHAPTER 5: Pivot Table and Vlookup — 91

Creating Excel Tables 91

Excel Table Benefits and Drawbacks 91

Preparing Your Data 92

Create an Excel Table 92

Sort and Filter the Data 93

Rename an Excel Table 94

Create Excel Table with Specific Style 95

Show Totals in a Table 96

Modify and Add Totals 97

Refer to any Table Column in a Formula 97

Formula Outside the Table 97

Add a Counter Field 99

Print Excel Table Only 99

Using Pivot Tables in Excel 99

The VLOOKUP Function 101

BONUS: 50 complex formulas to streamline your daily work — 107

CONCLUSION — 112

INTRODUCTION

Microsoft Excel is the most widely used spreadsheet software in the world, with millions of users. Excel and other spreadsheet programs are "excellent" for data manipulation, analysis, and visualization because they allow you to filter, chart, and format your data all in one program. Want to keep track of your grades and measure averages automatically? Are you considering gathering contact information for a field trip? Or assisting your students in writing a lab report? Excel is the program you'll need!

It is our responsibility to make sense of the data that is all around us. An added benefit is that you can work with anyone, and Excel assists you along the way! Collaborate in real-time with students and your colleagues, either for free using a lightweight online version of Excel or using the rich desktop software. Excel also includes intelligent analysis and support features to help you quickly comprehend your results.

Excel now has a lot of teamwork features that can help you get things done, no matter where your employees are based. MS Office is a truly global collection of tools. With Excel, we can share spreadsheets and have managers or team members add data, modify formulas, alter or add charts, and change existing cells and formatting. You can then monitor and manage the changes, accept or reject cell changes, and add comments to data cells as required.

The possibilities of working on a sheet with other colleagues are limitless with Office 365, which is now being rolled out to a large number of businesses. Collaboration through the internet is the way to go!

Excel Tools

There are several tools in Excel that have rendered it easier and more efficient to use. It has developed menus and tools to assist Excel users with further customizing their spreadsheets and workbooks. The easy access toolbar was designed to allow users to easily access commonly used commands. This toolbar can be customized using the Excel application, or a related workbook. Excel also created the "Ribbon" to substitute the original Excel menu templates. Users of Excel were able to tailor the belt to suit their specific needs.

File Formats That Are Supported in Excel

The format types or file types in Excel are crucial since they inform you about the files before you open them, and they and allow you to save them as macro-enabled files, binary files, templates, and so on. Furthermore, Microsoft Excel also introduced novel ways to save workbooks and other Excel applications. The "Import" and "Export" feature allows Excel users to easily import workbooks, data, and export workbooks or files that have been already created and can be used later.

.xlam	Excel Add-in	This is for Excel latest versions, Excel 2019, 2016, 2013, and Office Excel 2007, use the XML-based and macro-enabled Add-in format. An Add-in is an application that operates additional code in addition to the main programmed. VBA assignments and macro sheets Excel 4.0 are supported (.xlm).
.xls	Excel 97-Excel 2003 Workbook	This is a binary file format for Excel 97-2003.
.xls	Microsoft Excel 5.0/95 Workbook	This is a Binary file format for Excel 5.0/95.
.xlsb	Excel Binary Workbook	This is for Excel latest versions, Excel 2019, 2016, 2013, 2010, and Office Excel 2007, use the binary file format. This is a convenient load-and-save data format for those who need to load data files as quickly as possible. VBA assignments, macro sheets Excel 4.0, and many of Excel's latest updates are supported. However, since this isn't an XML file format, it's not ideal for viewing and editing information without Excel 2019, 2016, 2013, 2010, or 2007 and the object model.
.xlsm	Excel Macro-Enabled Workbook	This is for Excel 2021, 365, 2019, 2016, 2013, 2010, and 2007 use an XML-based and macro-enabled file format. Excel 4.0 macro sheets or VBA macro code are stored (.xlm).
.xlsx	Strict Open XML	It is a variant of an Excel Workbook file type that adheres to ISO standards

	Spreadsheet	(.xlsx).
.xlt	Excel 97-Excel 2003 Template	This is for an Excel template, the Excel 97 - Excel 2003 Binary file format is used.
.xltm	Excel Macro-Enabled Template	This is for the latest Excel versions, Excel 2019, 2016, 2013, 2010, and 2007 macro-enabled file format for an Excel template. VBA macro code or Excel 4.0 macro sheets are stored (.xlm).
.xltx	Excel Template	This is for the latest Excel editions, Excel 2019, 2016, 2013, 2010, and 2007. The default file format for an Excel prototype is.xlsx. VBA macro code and Excel 4.0 macro sheets cannot be saved (.xlm).
.xlw	Excel 4.0 Workbook	Only chart sheets, worksheets, and macro sheets are saved in this Excel 4.0 file format. In the latest Excel versions and Excel 2019, 2016, and 2013, users can open a workbook in this file format but are unable to save it.
.xml	Spreadsheet 2003XML	XML is a file format for spreadsheets.
.XPS	XPS FOR Document	The XML paper specification is a file format that retains text formatting while still allowing for file sharing. The XPS file contains the same structure that users expected when accessed online or printed, and the details in the file cannot be readily modified.

Terminologies of Excel

Workbooks

An Excel spreadsheet document is referred to as a workbook. The workbook saves all of the information and helps you to filter and measure the results.

A shared workbook is one that can be accessed and updated by several users on the same network.

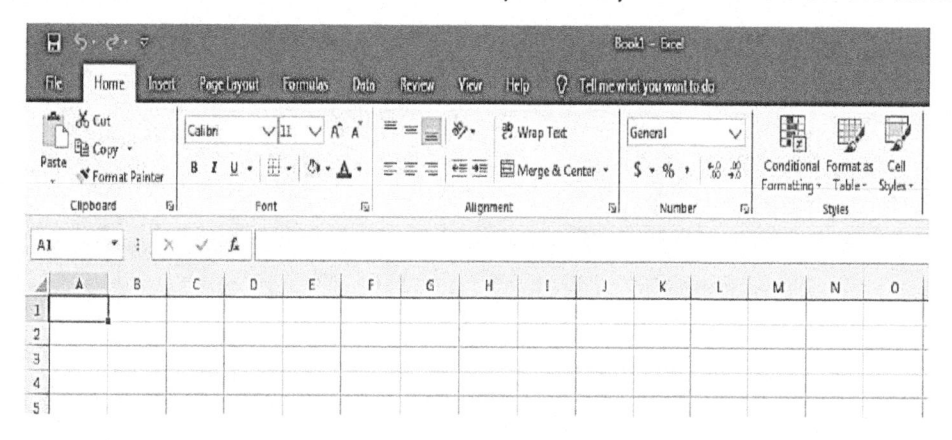

Worksheet

A worksheet is a text that is part of a workbook. Various sheets may be perched in a workbook, which is also known as a spreadsheet. Either of the worksheets you are currently working on is shown by tabs at the bottom of the page; it is also regarded as a dynamic sheet or current worksheet.

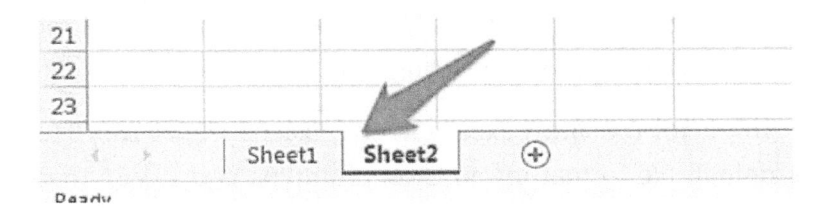

Cell

On a spreadsheet, a cell is the conjunction of a row as well as a column. In a spreadsheet, each cell could contain any attribute that could be accessed by a virtual cell relation or a formula. Any information you wish to use in your worksheet must be entered into a cell. A cell that is presently available for editing is known as an "active cell."

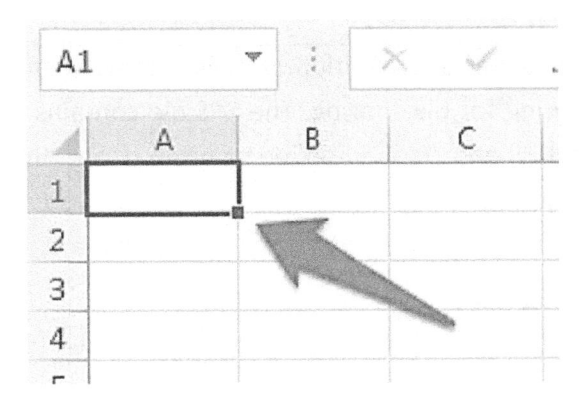

Rows and Columns

The alignment of the cells is described by columns and rows. The rows are horizontally spaced, while the columns are vertically oriented.

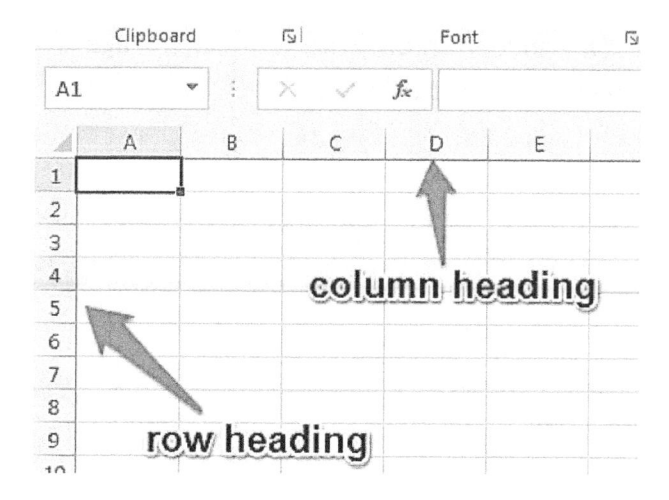

Rows Headings with Columns

The lettered and counted gray areas—which are just outside columns—and rows are the headings. When you tap on a heading, the whole row or column is selected. The headings may also be used to adjust the row height or column width.

Workspace

A workspace, as worksheets in a workbook, helps you access several files at once.

Ribbon

The "Ribbon" is a section of control tabs located just above the workbook. Behind every tab of the Ribbon is a plethora of choices.

Reference Cells

A cell reference is a sequence of parameters that defines a cell's classification. It is made up of letters and numbers. B3 will, for example, point to the cell at the intersection of column B as well as row 3.

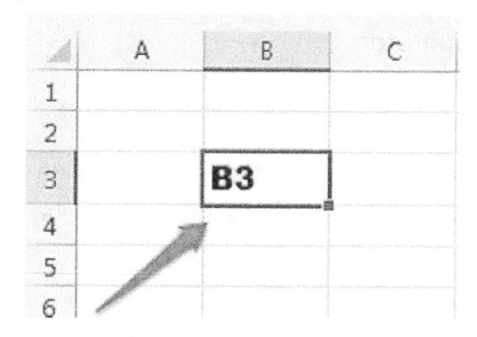

Range of Cells

A cell range is a set of cells that are being grouped together depending on a number of factors. Among cell references, use a colon (:). The range, also known as an array, could be determined by Excel. "A3: D3," for instance, would advise the formula to look at all cells in a box confined by columns C and F and rows 4 and 9, while "C4:F9" will indeed inform the formula to take a gander at all cells in a box surrounded by columns C as well as F, and rows 4 and 9.

Pivot Chart

Such a form of chart serves as a visual reference for pivot tables by displaying graphical representations of the data in the pivot table; the user may communicate with the data.

Region of Pivot

The pivot region is a spot on the worksheet in which you can move a pivot table field to change the appearance of a report.

Data Source

This is the data that went into making the pivot table. It may come from the worksheet itself or from an external database.

Values area

Value areas are the cells in a pivot table that hold the most up-to-date item. In the pivot table, these are sub-categories of fields. If you've got a country field, the items may be the United States of America, Italy, or other countries.

Template

A template is an Excel workbook or worksheet that has been designed to assist users in completing a given task. Stock research, operation maps, and calendars are examples of all this.

Operator

In an expression, operators are symbols and signs that determine which calculations to be performed. Operators don't have to become plain mathematical types; they may also be comparison, concatenation, text, or reference operators.

Formula

The term "formula" refers to a sequence of characters within a cell that is used to generate a value. It has to start with an equivalent sign (=). This may be a formula, a function, a cell relation, or an operator. An expression is another name for a formula.

Formula Bar

The formula bar is located in between the workbook as well as the Ribbon, and it displays the components of an active cell. In the context of formulas, the formula bar may show all the formula's elements.

Function

Functions are Excel calculations that have been pre-programmed. They're designed to make theoretically complicated calculations in a worksheet easier to understand.

Formatting Cells

That's the act of altering the appearance of a cell or its components in a spreadsheet. Just the visual representation of the cells is changed as you format them; the value inside the cells remains unchanged.

Error Code

If Excel detects an issue with a formula, "Error Codes" emerge.

Filtering

Filters are rules which you can use to determine which rows of a worksheet should be shown. Data like conditions or values may be used in these filters.

AutoFill

It makes it easy to copy data to several cells.

AutoSum

This feature adds up the figures in your sheet and shows the balance in the cell that you want.

AutoFormat

It is a program that applies a format to cells that meet those criteria. It may be as easy as a difference in height.

Validation of Data

Such a feature prevents unsuitable data from being inserted into the worksheet. Data authentication ensures that the data being entered is accurate and consistent.

Table Pivot

It is a data summarization method that is most often used to dynamically organize, aggregate, and sum data. The data is gathered from one table, and the findings are shown in another.

MS Excel Shortcut Keys

If you're familiar with Microsoft Excel, the amount and variety of keyboard shortcuts available to speed up your work and make things more convenient can surprise you.

Is anybody expecting you to remember any of these keyboard shortcuts? Certainly not! Since everyone's needs are unique, some would be more beneficial to you than others. It's worth it even though you just learn a few different tricks.

Workbook

Open/Create a new workbook	Ctrl + N
Open workbook	Ctrl + O
Save workbook	Ctrl + S
Save as	F12
Move/Go to the next workbook	Ctrl + Tab
Move/Go to the previous workbook	Ctrl + Shift + Tab
Minimize current workbook window	Ctrl + F9
Maximize current workbook window	Ctrl + F10
Protect the workbook	Alt + R, P W
Close current workbook	Ctrl + F4
Close Excel	Alt + F4

Ribbon

Collapse/Expand the ribbon	Ctrl + F1
Access keys activate	Alt
Shift/Move through groups & Ribbon tabs	→ ← ↑ ↓
Open or Activate selected control	Space or Enter
Confirm the control change	Enter
Go to the help on the selected control	F1

General

Ask for assistance	F1
Undo the previous activity	Ctrl + Z
Repeat the last action	F4
Cut the selected text	Ctrl + X

Display the Special Paste	Ctrl + Alt + V
Display find & replace with the Find tab chosen	Ctrl + F
Display find & replace with the Replace tab chosen	Ctrl + H
Find the previous match [after initial Find]	Ctrl + Shift + F4
Find the next match [after initial Find]	Shift + F4
Insert embedded chart	Alt + F1
Insert chart on a new sheet	F11
Toggle the Auto filter	Ctrl + Shift + L
Activate filter	Alt + ↓
Create table	Ctrl + T or Ctrl + L
Chose table row	Shift + Space
Chose table column	Ctrl + Space
Chose table [when the active cell is in table]	Ctrl + A
Filter for clear slicers	Alt + C
Run spellcheck	F7
Toggle thesaurus	Shift + F7
Open the macro dialog box	Alt + F8
Open VBA Editor	Alt + F11
Duplicate text, formula, or object	Ctrl + D
Select to the grid [whilst dragging]	Alt
Seen or hidden objects	Ctrl + 6
The Modify Cell Style dialogue box will appear	Alt + '
Show the right-click menu	Shift + F10
Display the control menu	Alt Space

Number Formatting

Use General format	Ctrl + Shift + ~
Use Number format	Ctrl + Shift + !

Use Time format	Ctrl + Shift + @
Use Date format	Ctrl + Shift + #
Use Currency format	Ctrl + Shift + $
Use Percentage format	Ctrl + Shift + %
Use Scientific format	Ctrl + Shift + ^

Drag & Drop

Pull/Drag and cut	Drag
Pull/Drag and copy	Ctrl + Drag
Pull/Drag and insert	Shift + Drag
Pull/Drag and insert copy	Ctrl + Shift + Drag
Pull/Drag to the worksheet	Alt + Drag
Pull/Drag to the duplicate worksheet	Ctrl + Drag

Navigation

Go/Move one cell right	→
Go/Move one cell left	←
Go/Move one cell up	↑
Go/Move cell down	↓
Go/Move one screen right	Alt + PgDn
Go/Move one screen left	Alt + PgUp
Go/Move one screen up	PgUp
Go/Move one screen down	PgDn
Go/Move to the right edge of the data region	Ctrl + →
Go/Move to the left edge of the data region	Ctrl + ←
Go/Move to the top edge of the data region	Ctrl + ↑
Go/Move to the bottom edge of the data region	Ctrl + ↓
Go/Move to the beginning of the row	Home
Go/Move to the last cell in the worksheet that contains	Ctrl + End

data	
Go/Move to the first cell in the worksheet	Ctrl + Home
Turn the End mode on	End

Selection

Choose/Select the entire row	Shift + Space
Choose/Select the entire column	Ctrl + Space
Choose/Select the current region if the worksheet contains data (press to select the current region and summary rows, and press to select the entire worksheet)	Ctrl + A
Expand the selection	Shift + Click
Add non-adjacent cells to selection	Ctrl + Click
Shift/Move to the right between the non-adjacent selections	Ctrl + Alt + →
Shift/Move to the left between the non-adjacent selections	Ctrl + Alt + ←
'Add to the "Selection" mode "Toggle"	Shift + F8
"Add to Selection" mode and "Exit"	Esc

Special Select

Show the "Go To" dialog box	Ctrl + G or F5
Choose/Select the cells with comments	Ctrl + Shift + O
Choose/Select the current region around the active cell	Ctrl + Shift + *
Choose/Select the current region	Ctrl + A
Choose/Select the direct precedents	Ctrl + [
Choose/Select all the precedents	Ctrl + Shift + {
Choose/Select the direct dependents	Ctrl +]
Choose/Select all the dependents	Ctrl + Shift +}
Choose/Select visible cells only	Alt +;

Cell Edit Mode

The active cell should be edited	F2
Add or delete a comment	Shift + F2
Remove the comment	Shift + F10, M
Cancel editing	Esc
Choose one character (right)	Shift + →
Choose one character (left)	Shift + ←
Shift one word (right)	Ctrl + →
Shift one word (left)	Ctrl + ←
Choose one word (right)	Shift + Ctrl + →
Choose one word (left)	Shift + Ctrl + ←
Choose to start the cell	Shift + Home
Choose to end the cell	Shift + End
Remove to the end of the line	Ctrl + Delete
Remove the character to the left of the cursor	Backspace
Remove the character to the right of the cursor	Delete
Start a new line in same cell	Alt + Enter

Entering Data

Enter data and move down	Enter
Enter data and move up	Shift + Enter
Enter data and move right	Tab
Enter data and move left	Shift + Tab
Enter data and stay in the same cell	Ctrl + Enter
Enter same data in multiple cells	Enter
Insert current date	Ctrl +;
Insert current time	Ctrl + Shift +:
Fill down from cell above	Ctrl + D

Fill right from the cell on left	Ctrl + R
Copy formula from cell above (exact copy)	Ctrl + '
Copy value from the cell above	Ctrl + Shift + "
Insert hyperlink	Ctrl + K
Display AutoComplete list	Alt + ↓
Flash fill	Ctrl + E

Formatting

Format cells	Ctrl + 1
Display Format Cells with Font tab selected	Ctrl + Shift + F
Add or remove bold	Ctrl + B
Add or remove Italics	Ctrl + I
Add or remove Underscore	Ctrl + U
Add or remove Strikethrough	Ctrl + 5
Align to the center	Alt + H, A C
Align to the left	Alt + H, A L
Align to the right	Alt + H, A R
Indent	Alt + H, 6
Remove the indent	Alt + H, 5
Wrap the text	Alt + H, W
Align the top	Alt + H, A T
Align the middle	Alt + H, A M
Align the bottom	Alt + H, A B
Increase the font size one step	Alt + H, F G
Decrease the font size one step	Alt + H, F K

Borders

Ribbon can show a list of border styles	Alt + H, B
Add a border across the cells you've selected	Ctrl + Shift + &

Add or remove right border	Alt + H, B R
Add or remove the left border	Alt + H, B L
Add or remove top border	Alt + H, B P
Add or remove the bottom border	Alt + H, B O
Add all the borders to all the cells in the selection	Alt + H, B A
Borders can be removed	Ctrl + Shift + -

Extend Selection

Extend selection (right)	Shift + →
Extend selection (left)	Shift + ←
Extend selection (up)	Shift + ↑
Extend selection (down)	Shift + ↓
The Extend selection to the last cell on the right or to the next cell or to the last column that contains data	Ctrl + Shift + →
The Extend selection to the last cell on the left or to the next cell, or to the first column that contains data	Ctrl + Shift + ←
The Extend selection to the last cell up or to the next cell or to the first row that contains data	Ctrl + Shift + ↑
The Extend the selection to the last cell down or to the next cell or to the last row that contains data	Ctrl + Shift + ↓
Extend selection (up one screen)	Shift + PgUp
Extend selection (down one screen)	Shift + PgDn
Extend selection (right one screen)	Alt + Shift + PgDn
Extend selection to the left one screen	Alt + Shift + PgUp
Extend selection to the start of rows	Shift + Home
Extend selection to the first cell in the worksheet	Ctrl + Shift + Home
Extend selection to the last cell in the worksheet	Ctrl + Shift + End
"Extend Selection" mode "Toggle"	F8
"Extend Selection" mode "Cancel"	Esc

Active Cell

Choose the working cell (when there are already several cells selected)	Shift + Backspace
Display the working cell on the worksheet	Ctrl + Backspace
Shift/Move the working cell clockwise to the corners of the selection	Ctrl + .
Shift/Move the working cell down in the selection (wrap to the next column)	Enter
Shift/Move up the working cell in the selection (wrap to the previous column)	Shift + Enter
Shift/Move the working cell in a selection to the right (wrap to the next row)	Tab
Shift/Move the working cell in a selection to the left (wrap to the previous row)	Shift + Tab

Formulas

Start by entering a formula	= or +
Toggled (in cell edit mode) relative and absolute references	F4
The Insert Function Dialog Box would display	Shift + F3
Auto sum	Alt + =
Switch on and off the display of formulas	Ctrl + `
Insert arguments to the function.	Ctrl + Shift + A
Filled in the array formula	Ctrl + Shift + Enter
Worksheets to calculate	F9
Calculate the active worksheet (operational)	Shift + F9
Force all worksheets to be calculated	Ctrl + Alt + F9
(in cell edit mode) Evaluate a part formula	F9
The formula bar expanded or collapsed	Ctrl + Shift + U
Dialog box for feature arguments to be displayed	Ctrl + A

Open the Name Manager application	Ctrl + F3
In rows, columns create name from values	Ctrl + Shift + F3
Paste the name into the formula	F3
Auto-complete accept feature	Tab

Columns & Rows

Show the Insert Dialog box	Ctrl + +
Add the selected number of rows	Ctrl + +
Add the selected number of columns	Ctrl + +
Show the Delete dialog box	Ctrl + -
Remove the selected number of rows	Ctrl + -
Remove the selected number of columns	Ctrl + -
Remove the contents of selected cells	Delete
Hide the columns	Ctrl + 0
Hide the rows	Ctrl + 9
Unhide the rows	Ctrl + Shift + 9
Group columns or rows with columns/rows selected	Shift + Alt + →
Ungroup columns or rows with columns/rows selected	Shift + Alt + ←
Show Group Dialog Box, no rows/cols selected	Shift + Alt + →
Show Ungroup Dialog Box	Shift + Alt + ←
Show or hide outline symbols	Ctrl + 8

CHAPTER 1:
Excel Cases
(Formatting Rows and Columns)

Entering, Editing, and Managing Data

In this section, you'll start working on the workbook. The skills outlined in this chapter are usually included in the preliminary stages of creating one or more worksheets in a workbook.

Entering Data

Manually inserting data into your worksheet is the first step in creating the workbook (as seen in the image below). The stages below explain how to type column headings throughout "Row 2" in a worksheet:

1. On your worksheet, go to cell A2 and click.
2. Type in the name of a month, for example.
3. Using the right cursor keys, transfer the cursor to the right. The term will be entered into cell A2, and the next cell on the right will be activated.
4. Click the right cursor key to create "Unit Sales."
5. Repeat step 4 with the terms "Average Price" and "Sales in Dollars."

Once you've typed your column headings in Row 2, check the image below and see how the worksheet might look. It's worth noting that the term "Price" in cell C2 isn't available. This is because the columns are too narrow to accommodate the entry that you typed.

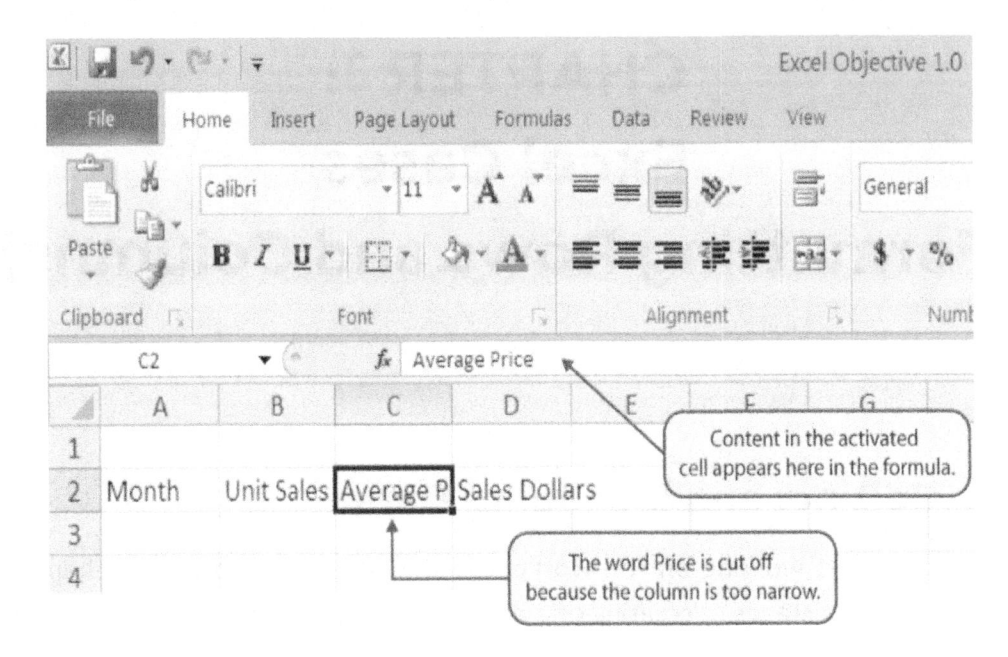

Entering Column Headings in a Worksheet

Column Headings

Column headings that correctly define the data inside a column of the worksheet are important. You'll almost certainly be sharing Excel workbooks among colleagues in a professional environment. Effective column headings minimize the risk of anyone misinterpreting the details in the worksheet, which could result in serious or even career-threatening mistakes.

1. Click cell B3.
2. Click the ENTER key, then type the number 2670. Cell B4 is activated after you click the ENTER key. Entering data down through a column with the ENTER key is a quick and productive method.
3. Enter the numbers 2160, 515, 1180, 1800, 590, 1030, 900, 775, 2875, 2700, and 3560 into cells B4 to B14.
4. Click cell C3.
5. Click the ENTER key after typing the number 9.99.
6. In cells C4 and C14, type 12.49, 14.99, 19.99, 17.49, 17.49, 14.99, 19.99, 9.99, 19.99, 19.99, 12.49, and 14.99.
7. Activate cell D3.
8. Click the ENTER key, then type the number 26685.
9. Enter the numbers 26937, 7701, 23562, 31416, 10269, 15405, 17958, 15708, 35916, 26937, and 53370 into cells D4 to D14.

When you've finished, double-check that the information you entered corresponds to the image below:

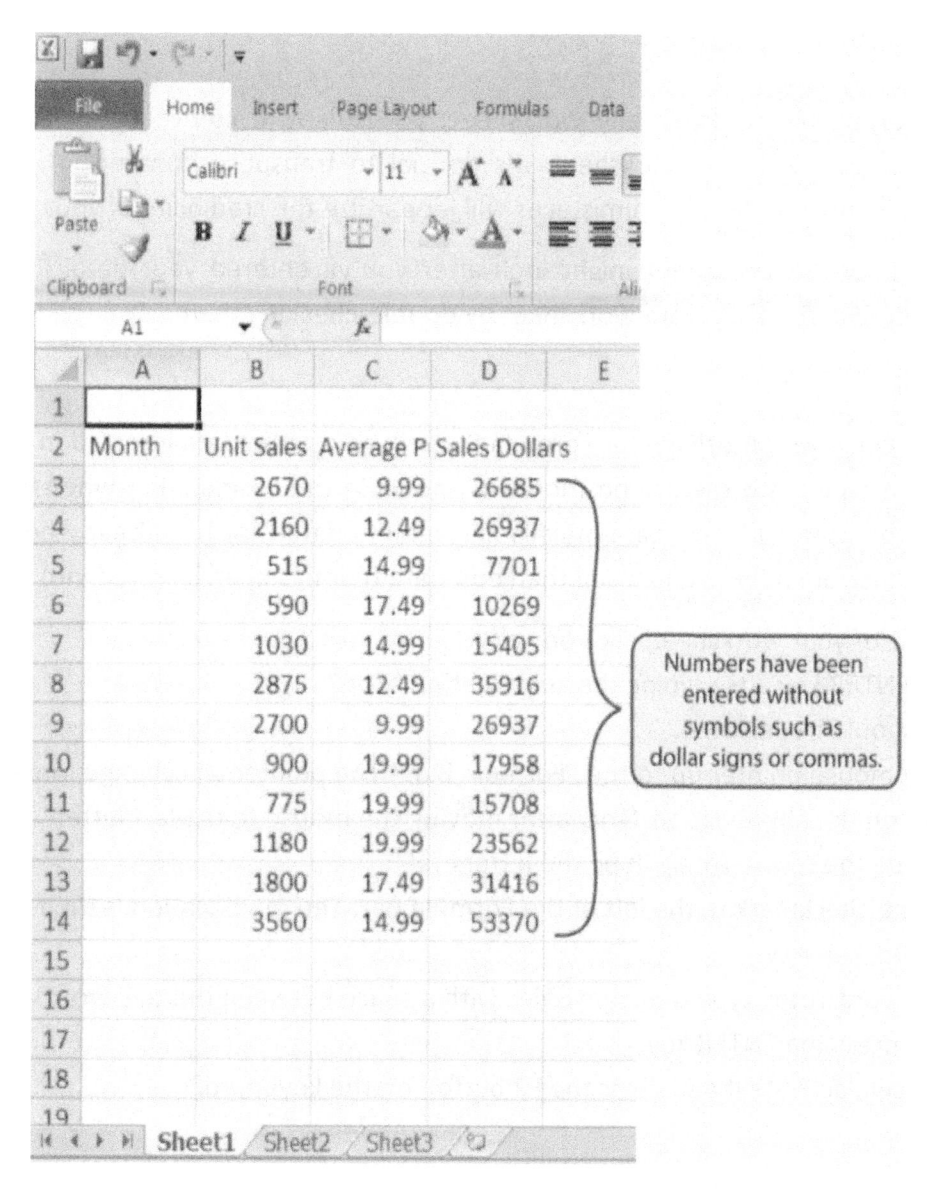

Completed Data Entry for Columns B, C, and D

Hint and Tips

While entering numbers, don't use symbols to format them.

It's safe not to use coding symbols like dollar signs and commas while entering numbers into an Excel worksheet. While you can incorporate these symbols when typing numbers in Excel, it delays the data entry operation. It's easier to apply these symbols to numbers after they've been typed into the worksheet using the formatting features of Excel.

Data Entry

It's critical to thoroughly proofread any worksheet, particularly if you've entered numbers. When manually inserting data into the worksheet, it's normal to transpose numbers. A number 563, for example, may be changed to 536. Such mistakes will jeopardize the credibility of your workbook.

Figure 2 depicts how the worksheet might look after you've entered your data. Please ensure the numbers are entered correctly in your worksheet by double-checking them.

Editing Data

Double-clicking a cell position using your Formula Bar will adjust the data inserted in it. You may have seen that the data typed into the cell position was shown in the Formula Bar when you typed it. The Formula Bar can be used to insert data in cells and modify data that has already been entered. The steps below demonstrate how to enter and then edit data that has been inserted into a cell position:

1. On Sheet 1 of your worksheet, click on cell A15.
2. Click the ENTER key after typing the abbreviation "Tot."
3. Cell A15 should be selected.
4. Move the mouse pointer up to the "Formula Bar." The pointer will change into the cursor. Left-click here on the abbreviation "Tot" after moving the mouse to the last letter.
5. To conclude the term "Total," type the letters "al."
6. Click on the checkmark to the left of the Formula Bar. The modification is then made in the cell.
7. Double-click cell A15.
8. After the word Total, type the word Sales with a space between the two words.
9. To begin, press the ENTER key.
10. To edit a cell, activate it and press the F2 button on the keyboard.

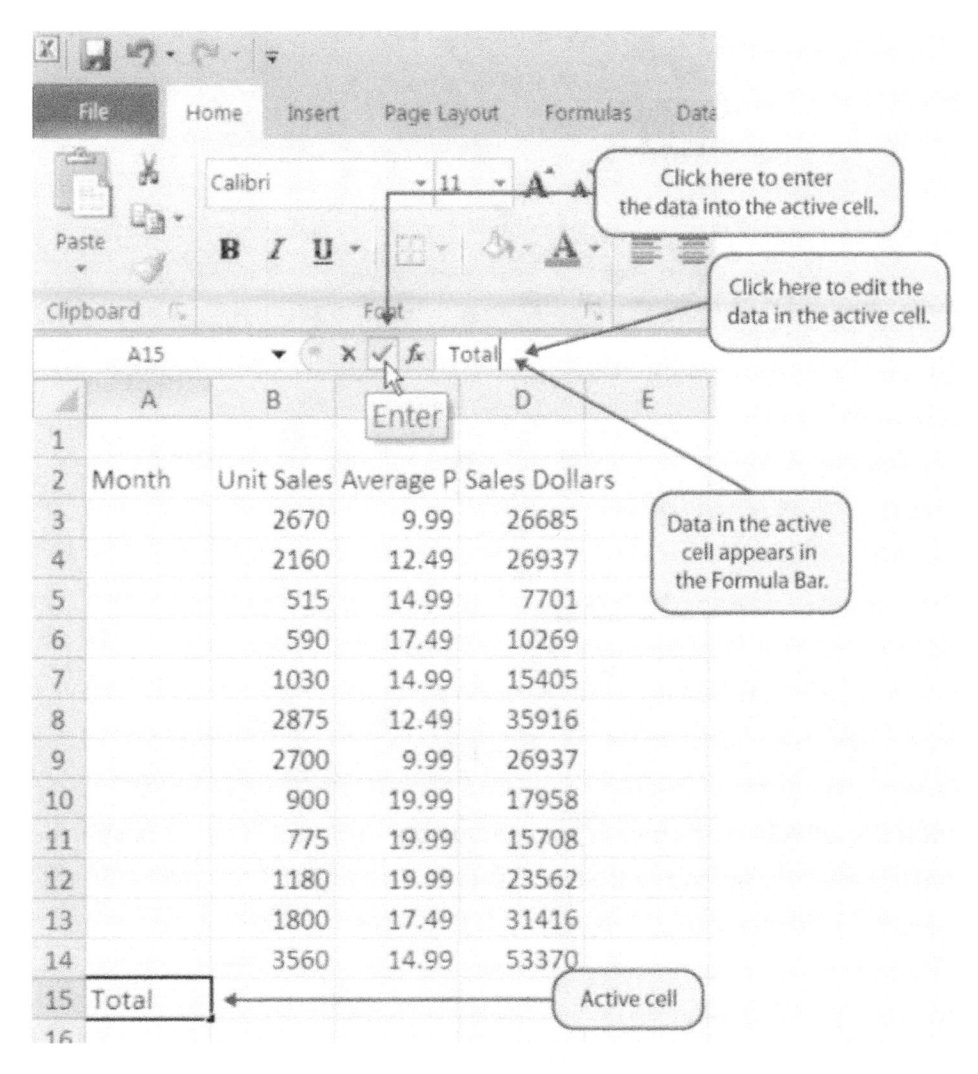

Using the Formula Bar to Edit and Enter Data

Auto Fill

When manually inserting data into a worksheet, the Auto Fill function comes in handy. This function is useful for various things, but it's especially useful when entering data in a certain order, like the numbers 1, 3, 5, 7, and so forth. It can even be used with non-numeric data like days of the week or months of the year. The stages below explain how to use Auto Fill to add certain months of a year in Column A:

1. On Sheet1 worksheet, click cell A3.
2. Click the "ENTER" key after typing the word "January."
3. Activate cell A3 again.
4. Move your mouse cursor to the bottom right corner of cell A3. In the corner of the cell, you'll see a tiny square called a "Fill Handle." The white plus sign of the block will transform into a black plus sign as the mouse cursor approaches the "Fill Handle."

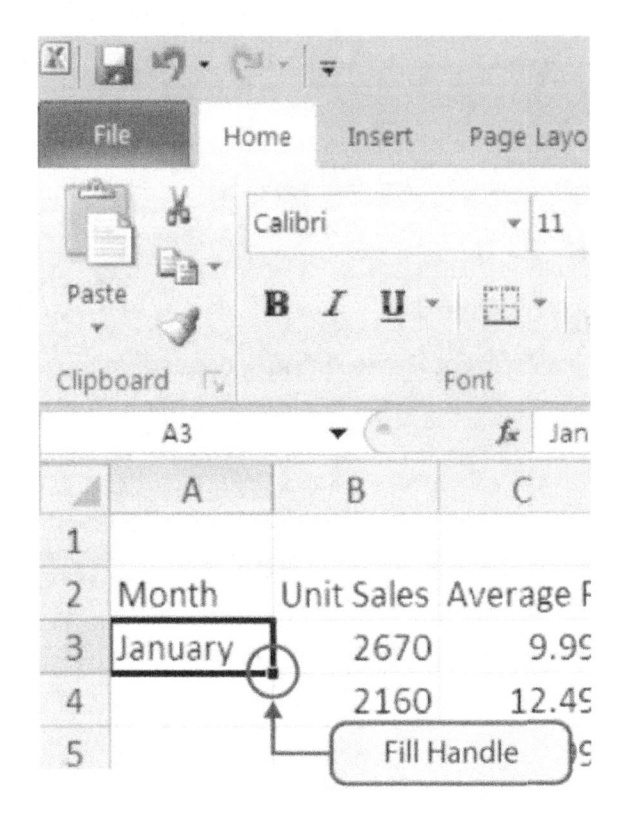

Drag the Fill Handle to cell A14 with the left mouse button. An AutoFill tips box specifies which month will be entered into every cell. When the tip box displays "December," remove your left mouse button.

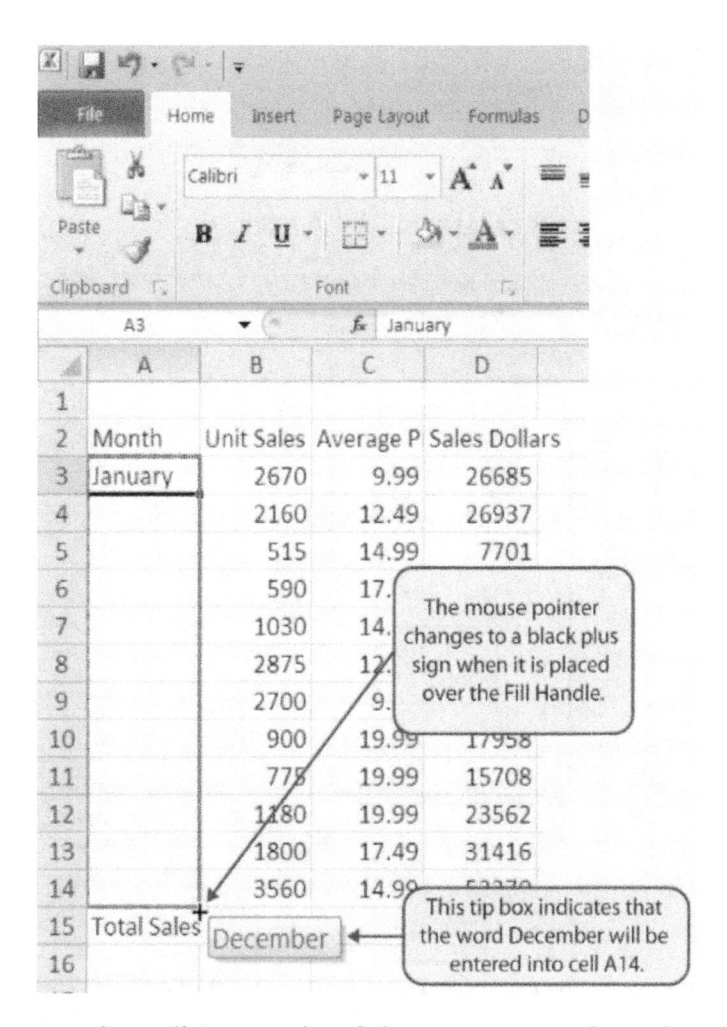

If you release your left mouse key, all 12 months of the year appear throughout the cell ranges A3:A14. An "Auto Fill Options" icon is also visible. You have many choices for inserting data into a collection of cells when you use this icon.

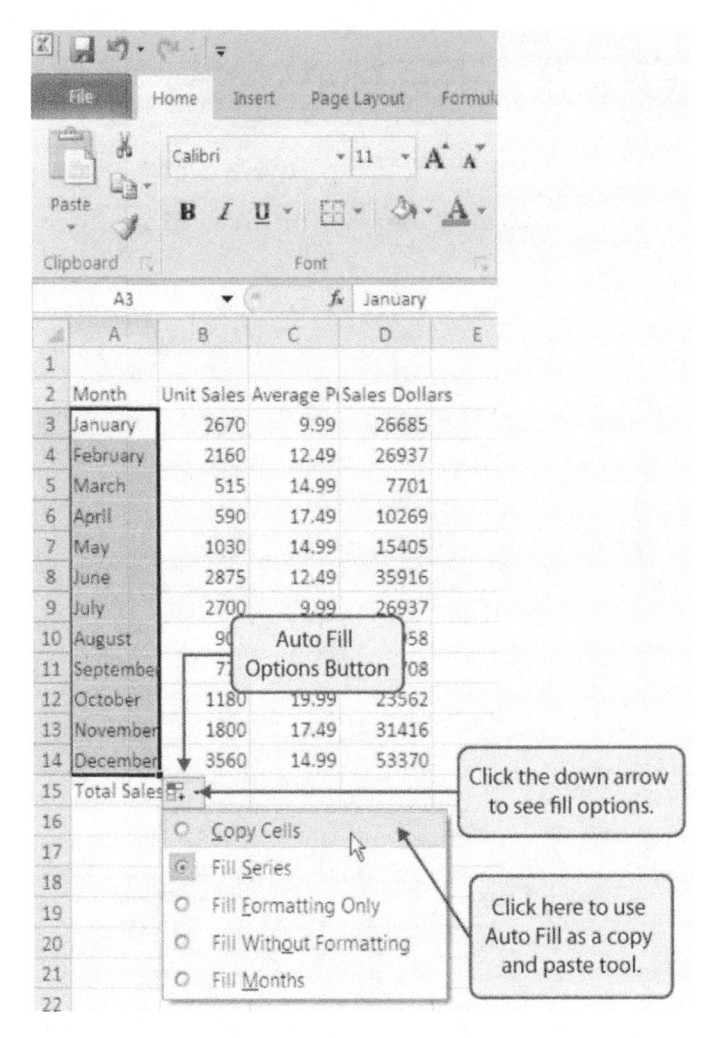

Auto Fill Options Button

1. Select "Auto-Fill Options" from the drop-down menu.
2. Select "Copy Cells" from the drop-down menu. The months into the range A4: A14 will then change to "January."
3. Click on the "Auto-Fill Options" tab again.
4. To restore all months of the year to the cell range A4: A14, select the "Fill Months" option. Choosing "Fill Series" achieves the same outcome.

Deleting Data and the Undo Command

There are a few strategies for removing data from a worksheet, and you'll explore some of them here. You can also use the "undo" command for each process.

This is a really useful command if you accidentally delete data from a worksheet. The steps below illustrate how to erase data from a cell or group of cells:

1. Place the mouse cursor over cell C2 and press the left mouse key to select it.

2. On the keyboard, press the "DELETE" key. The information in the cell is removed with this action.
3. Place the mouse cursor on cell C3 to highlight the group of cells C3:C14. Then, holding the left mouse button, drag down to the C14 cell.
4. Place your cursor over the Fill Handle. A white block plus sign will be replaced by a black plus sign.
5. Move up to cell C3, and click and drag your mouse cursor. Release the mouse key. The contents of the C3:C14 cell range will be erased.
6. This should replace the data back in the C3:C14 range.
7. Click the "Undo" button again. This should replace the information in cell C2.

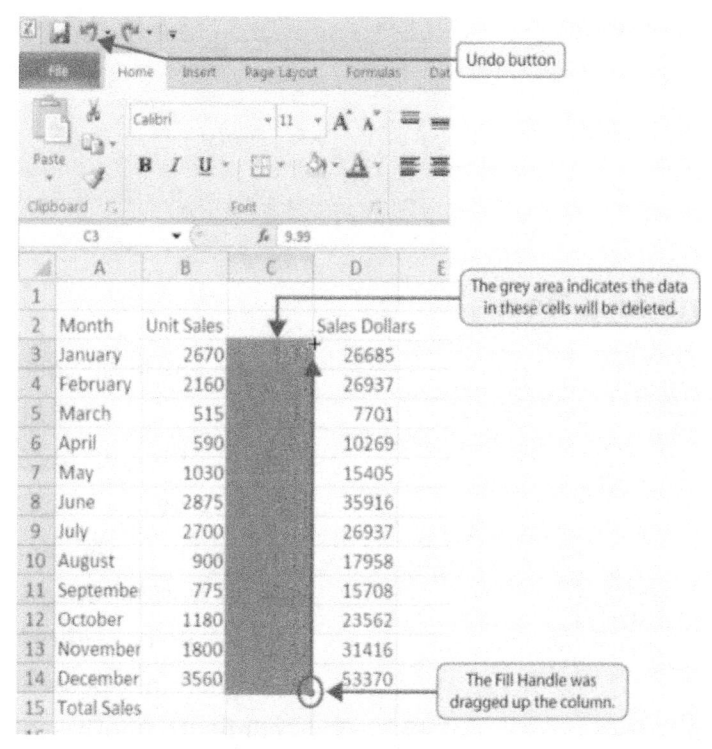

Keyboard Shortcuts for Command Undo

1. When pressing the letter "Z" on the keyboard, hold down your "CTRL" key.
2. Place the mouse cursor over cell C2 to highlight the C2:C14 range. Then, holding the left mouse button, drag the cursor down to cell C14.
3. In the "Ribbon Home" tab, next to the Cells group of the commands, click on the "Clear" button. This shows the drop-down menu with several choices for clearing or deleting data from a cell. You can also choose to clear the format of a cell or all hyperlinks in a cell.
4. Select "Clear All." This clears the data from the selected cell set.
5. To undo a change, press the "Undo" key. This replaces the data throughout the C2:C14 range.

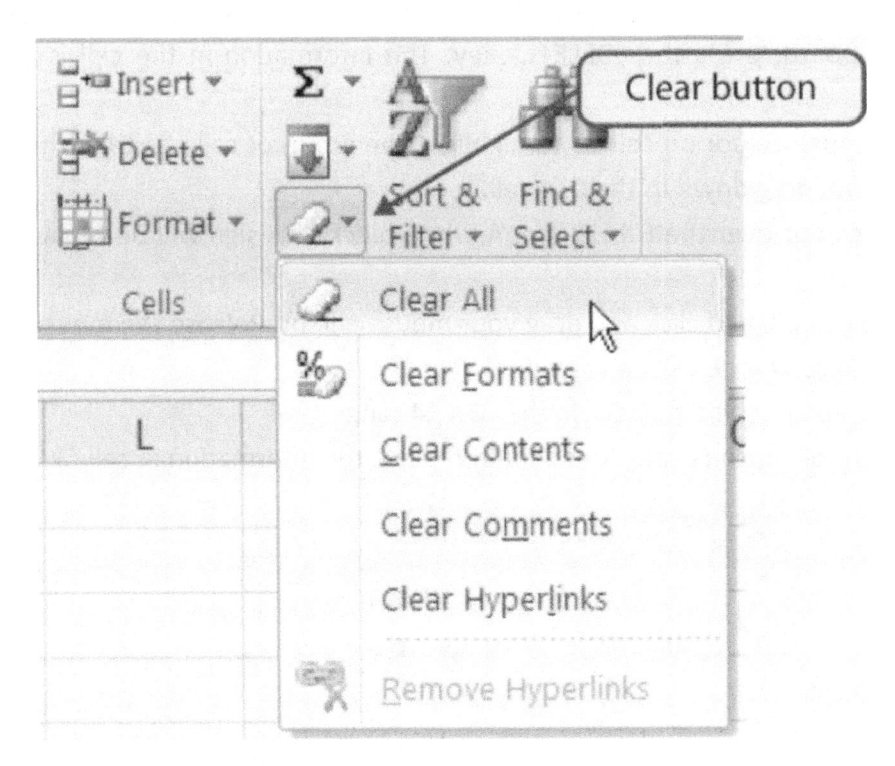

Adjusting Columns and Rows

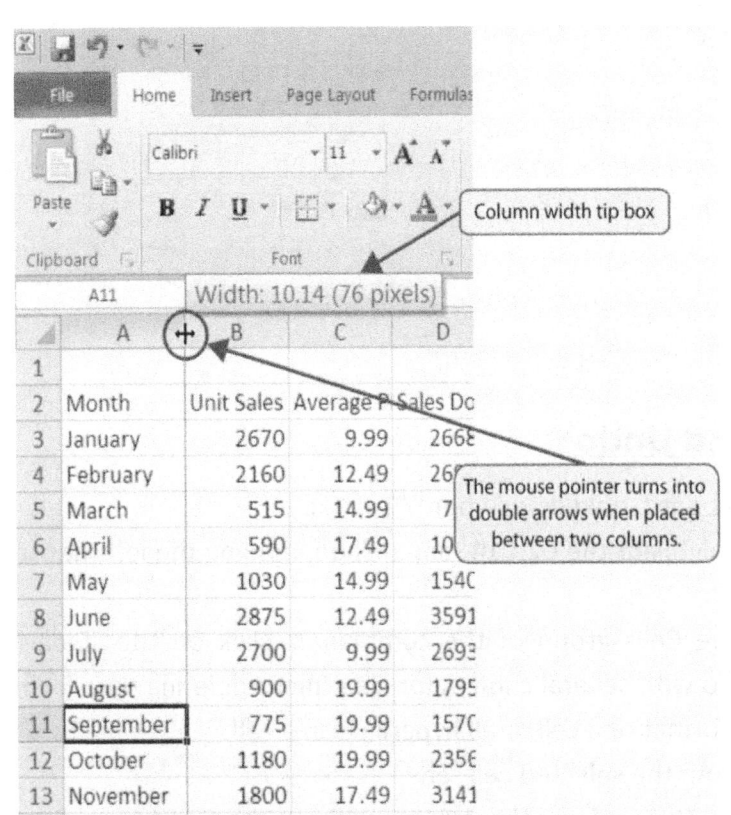

Some entries in your worksheet happen to be missing. In cell A11, for instance, the final letter of the word "September" is not visible. This is because the column is small for this expression. The columns and rows of the Excel worksheet can be rearranged to suit the data being entered into a cell. The instructions below will illustrate how to configure both column widths and row heights in a worksheet.

1. In the worksheet named Sheet1, slide the mouse cursor between Column A and Column B. A white block plus sign transforms into double arrows.

2. To see the whole word "September" in the A11 cell, click and move the column to the right. The column width tip box will appear as you move the column. The character's number would fit into the column using "Calibri 11-point" font, which is the default font/size configuration and is shown in this box.

30 | EXCELL ACCELERATOR

3. Release the left mouse key.

If you want to set the width of a specific character for one or more columns, you will notice that the "click-and-drag" approach is inefficient. By utilizing a certain number of characters, the following steps demonstrate a second approach to change the column widths:

1. By sliding the mouse cursor over the cell position and pressing the left mouse key, you can choose every cell location in Column A. If you want to set a similar character width for more than one column, you can highlight the locations of cells in many columns.
2. Left-click the "Format" button in the group of cells on the "Ribbon Home" tab.
3. From the drop-down menu, select the "Column Width" option. The Column Width dialog box will appear.
4. In the Column Width dialog box, type "13" and press the "OK" icon. This sets the character width in Column A to this value.
5. Bring your mouse cursor back between Columns A and B until a double arrow cursor appears; the double arrow is displayed when activating AutoFit. The column width is adjusted depending on the maximum entry set for the column.
6. Reset the column width to 13 using the Column Width dialog box.

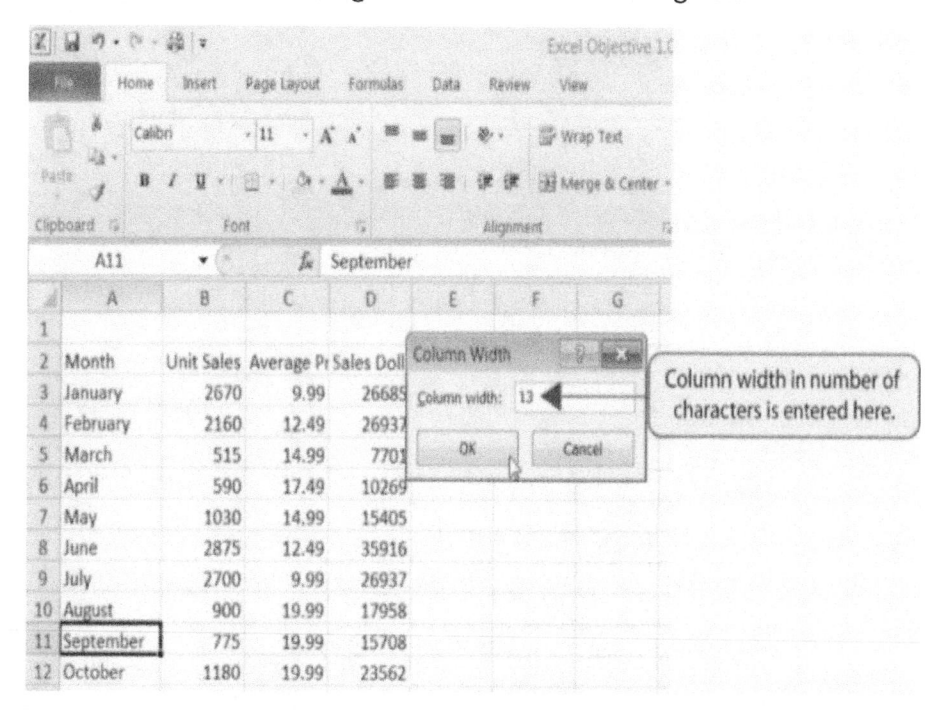

Keyboard Shortcuts for Column Width: Click the ALT key, then type the letters O, H, and W once on the keyboard.

Steps 1 to 4 explain how to change the height of a row, which is equivalent to changing the width of a column:

1. Place the mouse cursor over cell A15 and press the left mouse key to select it.
2. Left-click on the Format button of the group of cells on the Ribbon Home tab.
3. From the drop-down menu, select the Row Height option. The Row Height dialog box will appear.
4. Inside this Row Height dialog box, type 24 and press the OK icon. Row 15 will now have a height of 24 points. Each point is roughly 1/72 of an inch in size. This change in row height was created to make room between the worksheet's totals and the remainder of the results.

Keyboard Shortcuts for Row Height: Click the "ALT" key, then the letters "O," "H," and "H" once on the keyboard.

The image below depicts the worksheet after row 15 and column A had been modified.

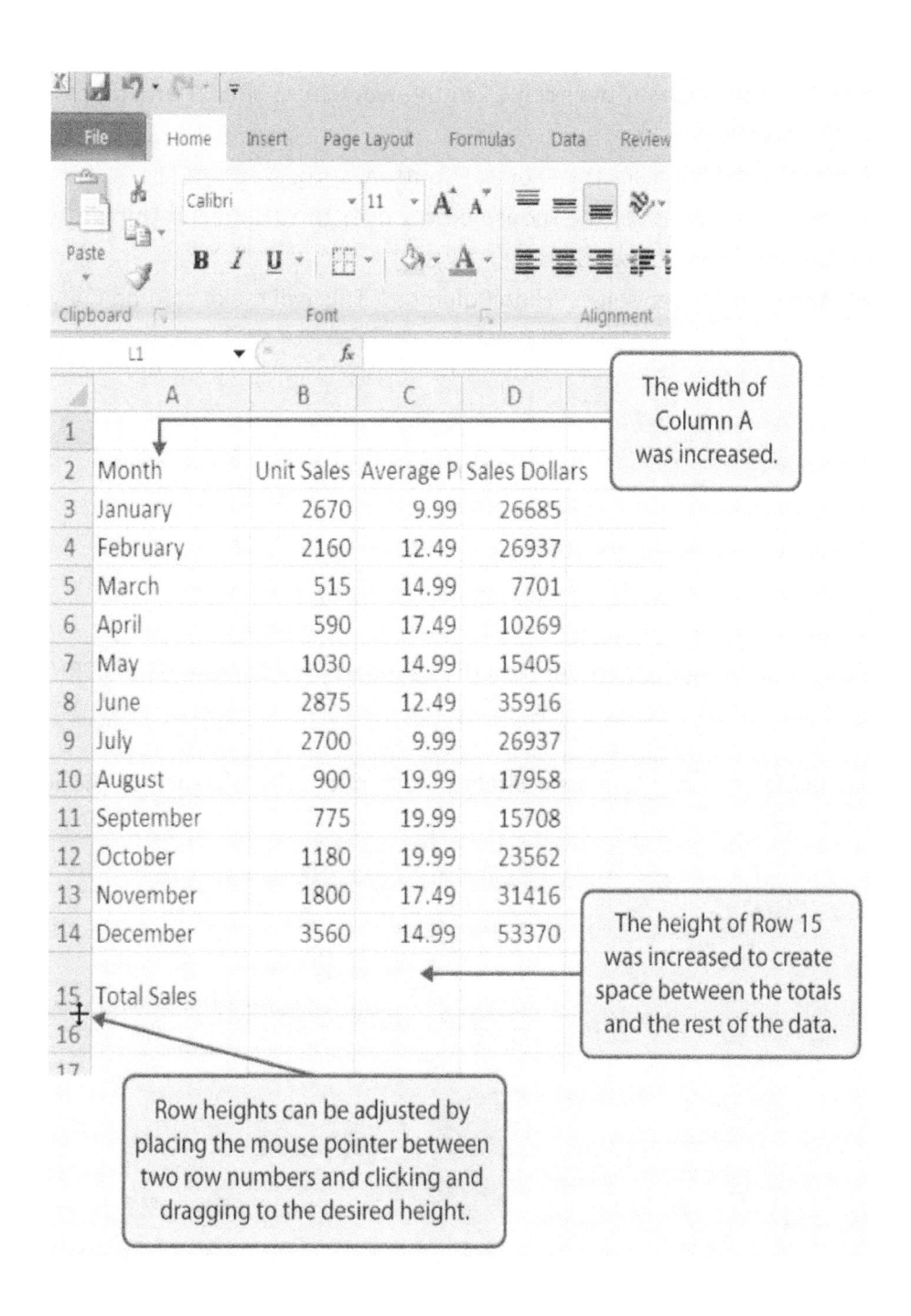

[Screenshot of Excel worksheet showing monthly sales data with columns for Month, Unit Sales, Average Price, and Sales Dollars from January through December, with a Total Sales row at row 15. Annotations indicate: "The width of Column A was increased.", "The height of Row 15 was increased to create space between the totals and the rest of the data.", and "Row heights can be adjusted by placing the mouse pointer between two row numbers and clicking and dragging to the desired height."]

Month	Unit Sales	Average P	Sales Dollars
January	2670	9.99	26685
February	2160	12.49	26937
March	515	14.99	7701
April	590	17.49	10269
May	1030	14.99	15405
June	2875	12.49	35916
July	2700	9.99	26937
August	900	19.99	17958
September	775	19.99	15708
October	1180	19.99	23562
November	1800	17.49	31416
December	3560	14.99	53370
Total Sales			

Hiding Columns and Rows

You can hide rows and columns on a worksheet in addition to changing them. This is a helpful strategy for improving the graphic presentation of your worksheet with data that doesn't need to be displayed. The workbook containing data on "GMW Sales" is used to illustrate these capabilities. This worksheet, however, does not include concealed rows or columns. These skills are only used for presentation purposes here:

1. By hovering the mouse cursor over cell C1 in the worksheet Sheet1 and tapping the left mouse key, you will access it.
2. In the "Ribbon Home" tab, click the "Format" button.
3. In the drop-down menu, hover the mouse cursor over the "Hide and Unhide" options. This will reveal a drop-down menu of options.
4. In your submenu of options, select "Hide Columns." This will make column C invisible.

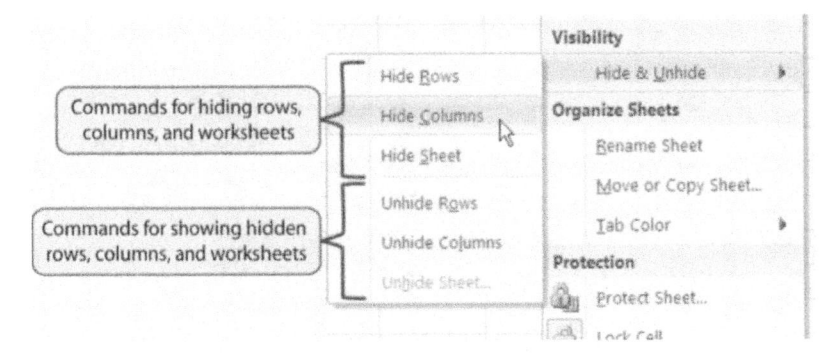

Hiding Columns: While pressing the number 0 on the keyboard, hold down your "CTRL" key.

The workbook has hidden column C in your Sheet1 worksheet. The absence of the letter C indicates that this column is concealed.

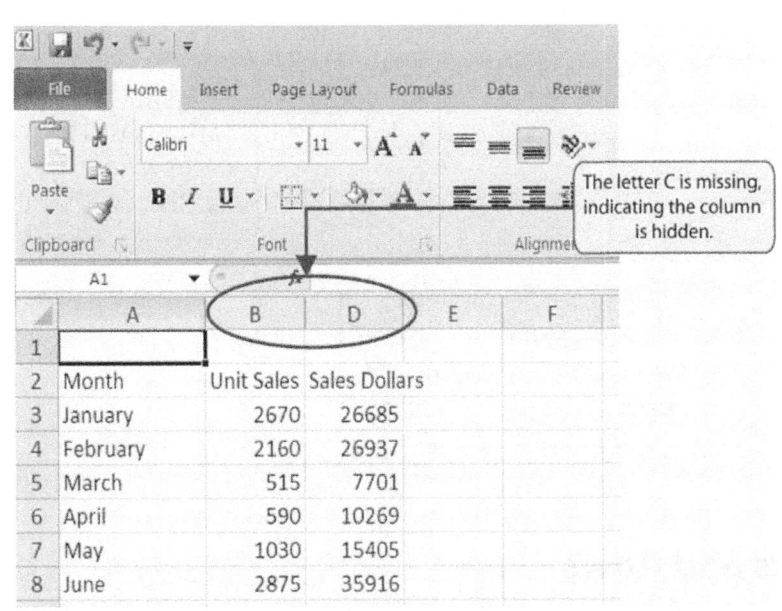

Hidden Column

Follow these steps to unhide the column:

1. By clicking on and holding cell B1 and dragging it into cell D1, you will highlight the B1:D1 range.
2. On the "Ribbon Home" tab, click on the "Format" icon.

3. "Unhide Columns" can be found in the sub-menu of options. On your worksheet, column C is then visible again.

Keyboard Shortcuts for Unhiding Columns: Hold down your "CTRL" and "SHIFT" keys while pressing the open parenthesis "(" key on the keyboard to highlight the cells on each side of a hidden column.

The steps below explain how you can hide rows in the same way as you can hide columns:

1. By hovering the mouse cursor over cell A3 in your Sheet1 worksheet and pressing the left mouse key, you will access it.
2. In the "Ribbon Home" tab, click on the "Format" key.
3. In the drop-down menu, hover the mouse cursor over the "Hide and Unhide" options. This will reveal a drop-down screen of options.
4. Hide Rows can be found in the sub-menu of the new list of options. This would make row 3 invisible.

Keyboard Shortcuts for Hiding Rows: When pressing the number 9 on the keyboard, hold down the CTRL key. Follow these steps to unhide the row:

1. By clicking on and holding cell A2 and dragging it to cell A4, the A2:A4 range is highlighted.
2. On the "Ribbon Home" tab, click on the "Format" key.
3. "Unhide Rows" can be found under the "Options" submenu. On your worksheet, row 3 will now be visible again.

Keyboard Shortcuts for Unhiding Rows: Hold down your CTRL and SHIFT keys when clicking the open parenthesis key "(" on the keyboard to highlight the cells above and below the hidden row(s).

Hidden Rows and Columns

In most professions, it is common for employees to use Excel workbooks created by coworkers. Often check for hidden columns and rows when using a workbook created by others. If a column letter or row number is absent, you will easily see if a column or row has been hidden.

Hiding columns and rows:

1. Activate a minimum of one cell in hidden column(s) or row(s).
2. Select the "Ribbon Home tab."
3. In the group of cells, click on the "Format" button.
4. Place your cursor over the "Hiding and Unhide" options.
5. Select "Hide Columns" or "Hide Rows" from the drop-down menu.

Unhiding columns and rows:

1. Cells above and below the hidden row(s) or to the left and right of a hidden column(s) are highlighted.
2. Select the "Ribbon Home" tab.

3. In the cells group, click on the "Format" key.
4. Place the cursor over the "Hide and Unhide" options.
5. Select "Unhide Columns" or "Unhide Rows" from the drop-down menu.

Inserting Columns and Rows

Using pre-made Excel workbooks is a time-saving method of working since it removes the need to build data worksheets from scratch. However, you will discover that you may have to add further rows or columns of data to achieve your objectives. In this scenario, you need to build a worksheet with blank rows or columns. The steps below explain how to do this:

1. You can access it by hovering the mouse cursor over cell C1 in your Sheet1 worksheet and pressing the left mouse key.
2. In the "Ribbon Home" tab, click the down arrow on the "Insert" icon.

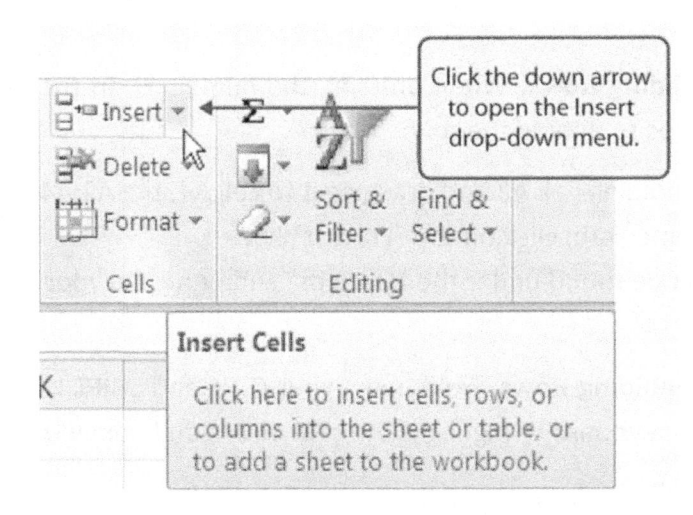

Insert Button

From the drop-down menu, select "Insert Sheet Columns." To the left of column C, a vacant column has been included.

Column D also contains the details that were originally in column C. It's worth noting that columns often are placed to the left of an active cell.

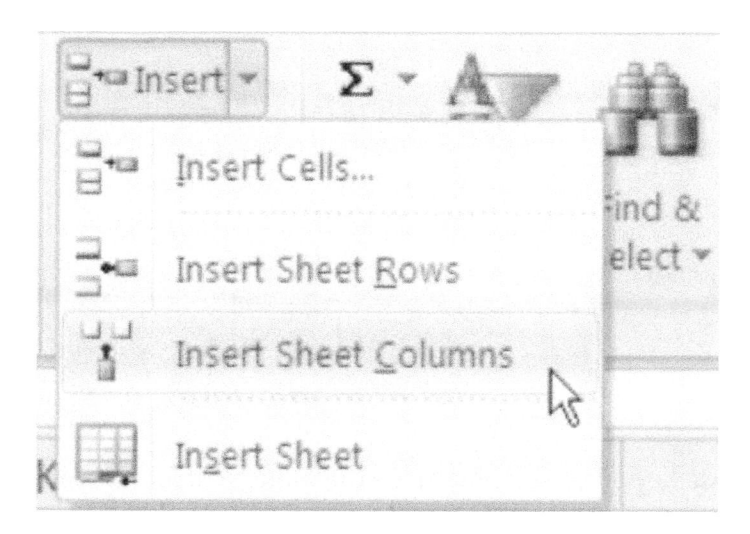

Insert Drop-Down Menu

Keyboard Shortcuts for Inserting Columns: After holding your "ALT" key, press the letters "I," "H," and "C" at once. Another column is added to the left of the active cell.

Inserting Columns

1. You will access it by hovering the mouse cursor over cell A3 in your Sheet1 worksheet and pressing your left mouse key.
2. In the "Ribbon Home" tab, click the down arrow until you reach the "Insert" key.
3. From the drop-down menu, select "Insert Sheet Rows." Over row 3, a vacant row has been added. Row 4 also contains the details that were originally in row 3. It's worth noting that rows are often placed over an active cell.

Keyboard Shortcuts for Inserting Rows: Holding the "ALT" key, press letters "I," "H," and "R" together. A row is added above the active cell.

Inserting Columns and Rows

1. Activate any cell to the right of or below the required, blank row or column.
2. Select the "Ribbon Home" tab.
3. In the group of cells, click the down arrow until you reach the "Insert" button.
4. Select either "Insert Sheet Row" or "Insert Sheet Column" from the drop-down menu.

Moving Data

You might want to transfer data in a worksheet to various positions after it has been entered. The measures below explain how to transfer data from one location on the worksheet to another:

1. By activating cell D2 and dragging it down to cell D15, you will highlight the D2:D15 range.
2. Bring your mouse cursor to the left of cell D2. You can see a white block plus symbol change to crossed arrows. This means that you can left-click the data and move it to a new location.

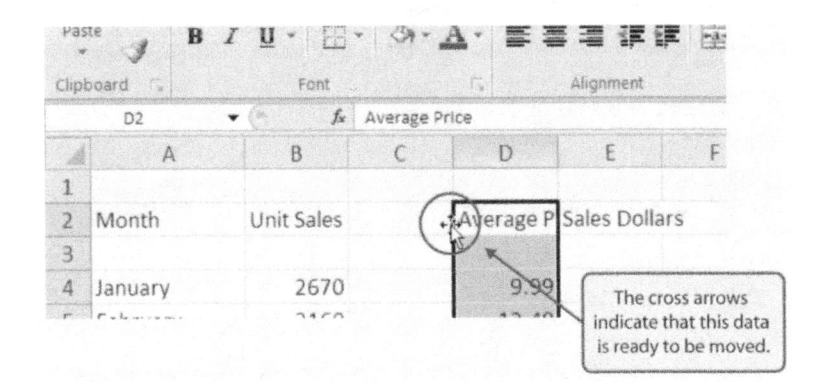

3. Click the left mouse key on cell C2 and move the mouse cursor.
4. Release your left mouse key. Column C now contains the details.
5. Using the "Quick Access Toolbar," click the "Undo" button. This returns the data to column D.
6. When you move data around on a worksheet, double-check that you've identified all the components related to the sequence you're transferring.
7. If you're transferring a column of information, for instance, ensure that the column heading has been included. Before moving a list, double-check that the values you need are illuminated.

Deleting Columns and Rows

You may need to erase whole rows and columns of content from a worksheet. This might be needed if you want to delete blank rows or columns from the worksheet or data-filled columns and rows. A method for extracting cell data can be utilized to remove unnecessary information.

If you don't want a vacant column or row in the workbook, you can remove it by following the steps below:

1. By hovering the mouse cursor over cell A3 and pressing the left key, you can access it.
2. In the "Ribbon Home" tab, click the down arrow until you reach the "Delete" button in the group of cells.
3. From the drop-down menu, choose "Delete Sheet Row." Row 3 is removed, and all data within the worksheet is shifted up one row.

Keyboard Shortcuts for Deleting Rows: Hold the "ALT" key, then press the letters "D," "H," and "R" together. The row in which the active cell is located is removed.

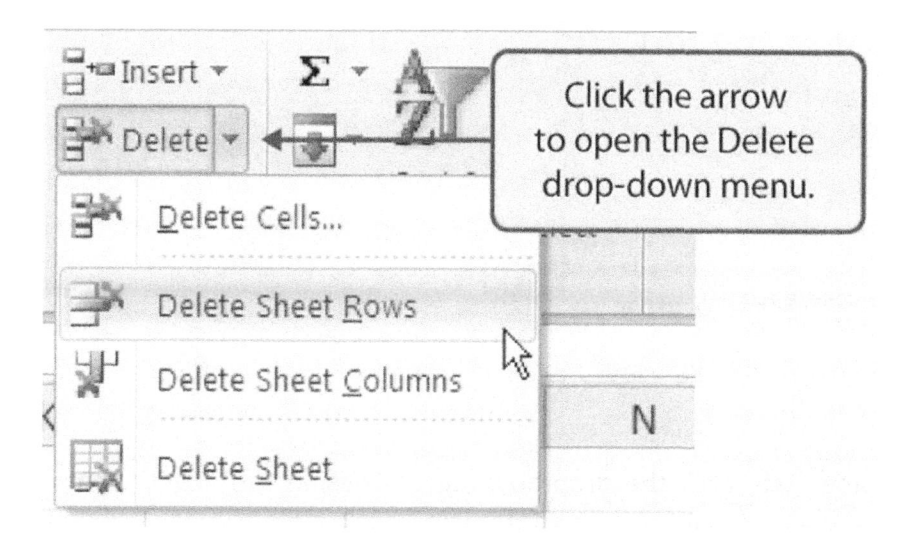

Delete Drop-down Menu

1. You can access it by hovering the mouse cursor over cell C1 and pressing the left button.
2. In the "Ribbon Home" tab, click the down arrow until you reach the Delete button in the group of cells.
3. From the drop-down menu, choose "Delete Sheet Column." Column C is removed, and all the content in your worksheet is shifted one column to the left.
4. Save your workbook modifications by pressing the "Save" icon on your "Home" ribbon or, alternatively, choosing "Save" from your "File" menu.

Formatting Cells

Simple formatting will help you personalize the look and feel of the workbook, helping you to highlight sections and make the text easy to read and comprehend. You could also use number formatting to tell Excel what kind of data you are working on within a workbook, like currency ($), percentages (%), and so on.

Changing the Font

Any new workbook font is adjusted to Calibri by default. On the other hand, in Excel, you can style your title cell like the illustration below to make it different from the rest of the worksheet.

1. Choose the cell(s) you would like to alter.

2. On the "Home" tab, click the drop-down arrow beside the "Font" command. A drop-down menu for fonts will appear.
3. Choose the font you want to use. As you move your cursor over multiple options, a live demonstration of the respective font appears. You'll use "Georgia" as an example.

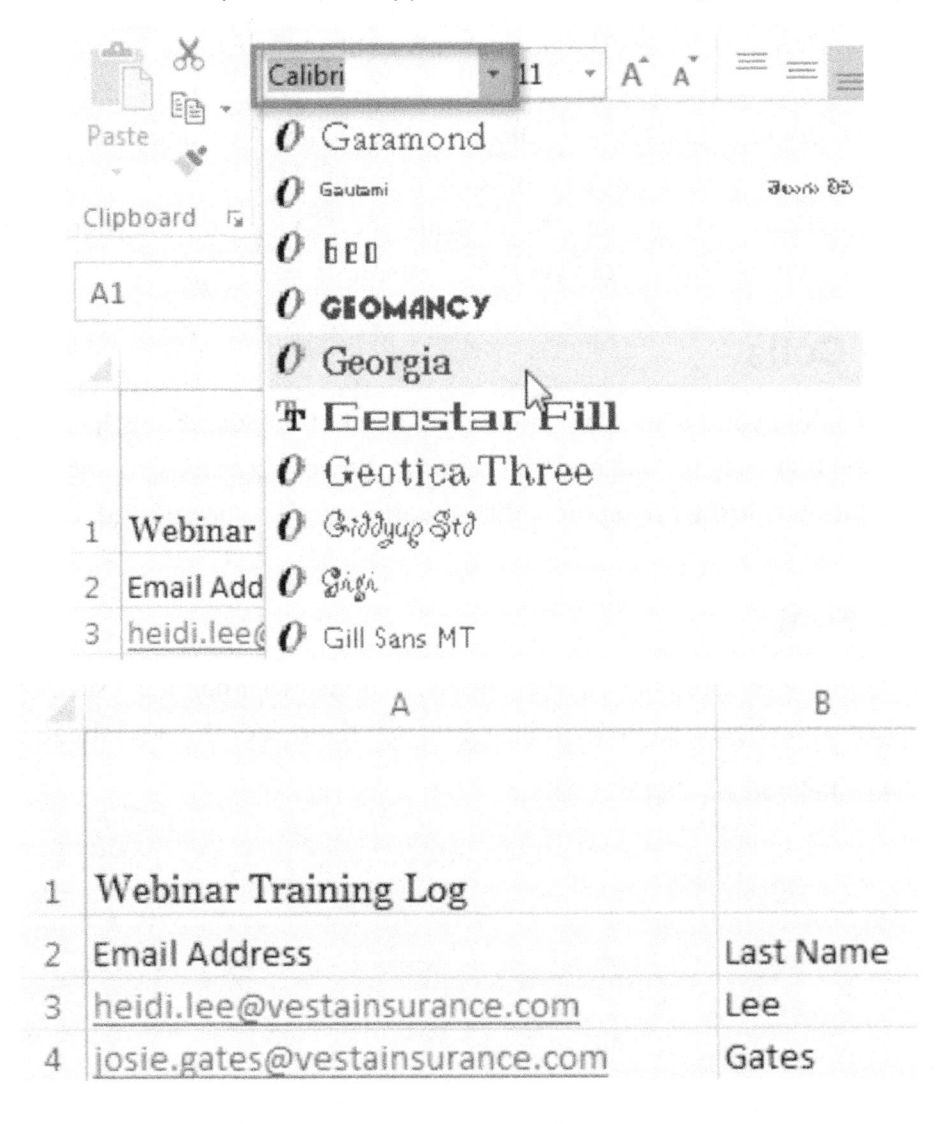

The text adjusts to the font you've chosen.

4. When making a workbook at work, use a font that is simple to understand. The normal reading fonts include Times New Roman, Cambria, and Arial, in addition to Calibri.

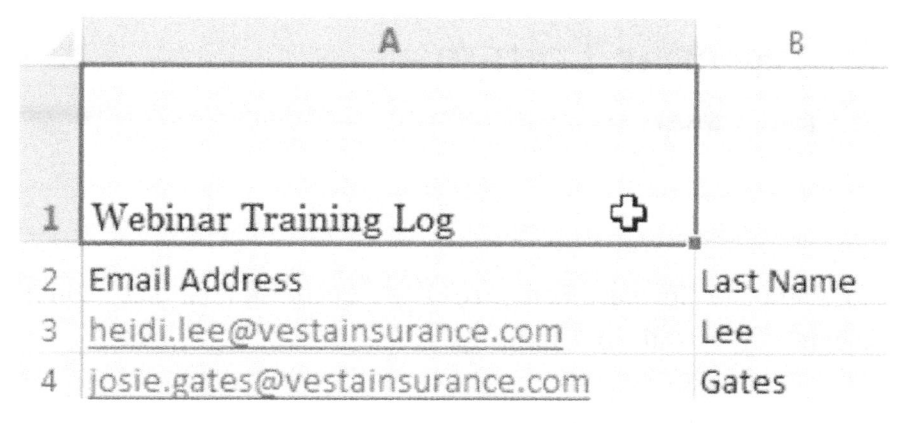

	A	B
1	Webinar Training Log	
2	Email Address	Last Name
3	heidi.lee@vestainsurance.com	Lee
4	josie.gates@vestainsurance.com	Gates

5. To change font size, choose the font size you want. As you move your cursor over various choices, a live demonstration of the respective font size appears. In this case, you'll use the number 16 to make the text bigger.

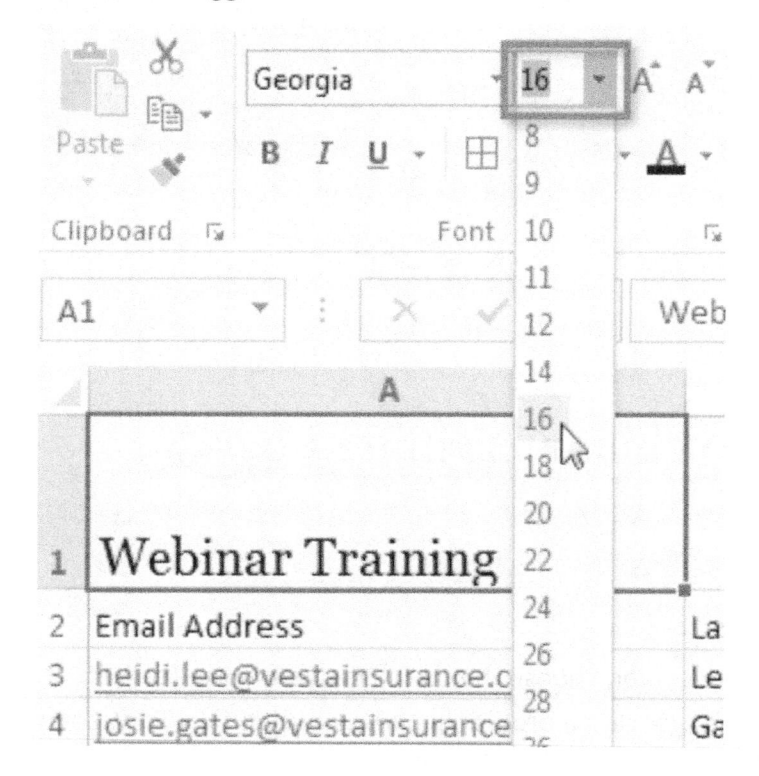

	A	B
1	Webinar Training Log	
2	Email Address	Last Name
3	heidi.lee@vestainsurance.com	Lee
4	josie.gates@vestainsurance.com	Gates

6. You can also utilize the "Increase Font Size" and "Decrease Font Size" commands or use your keyboard to enter any specific font size.

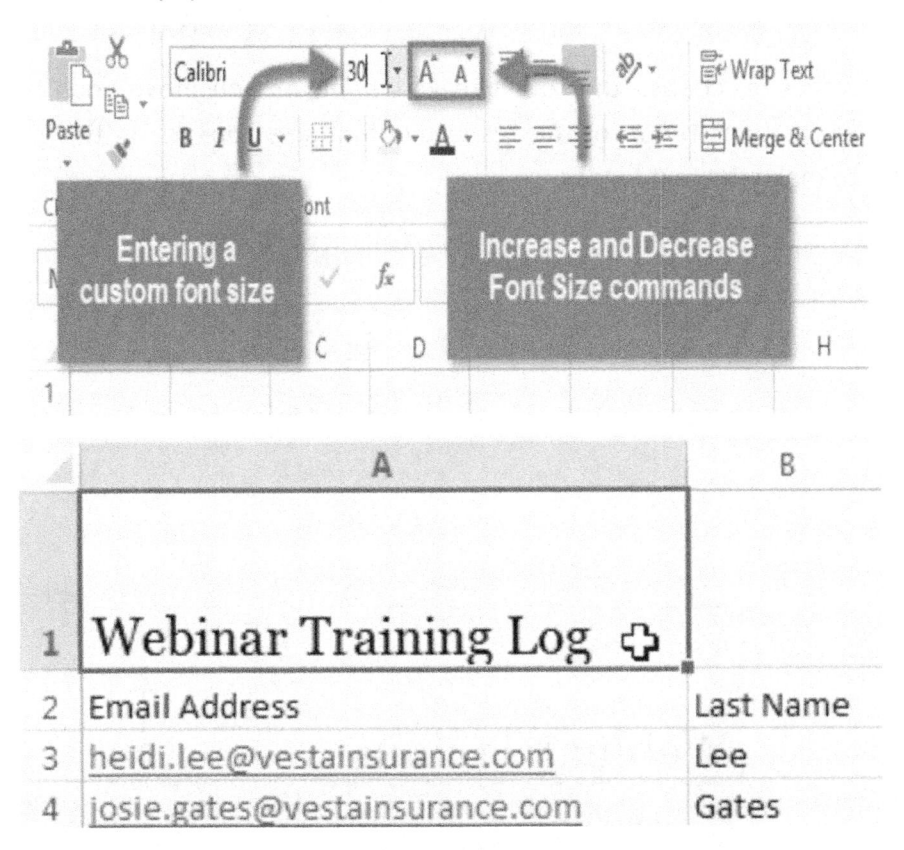

Entering a custom font size

Increase and Decrease Font Size commands

	A	B
1	Webinar Training Log	
2	Email Address	Last Name
3	heidi.lee@vestainsurance.com	Lee
4	josie.gates@vestainsurance.com	Gates

7. To change your font color, choose the cell(s) you would like to alter.
8. On your "Home" page, click a drop-down arrow beside the "Font Color" command. The "Color" menu will appear.
9. Choose the font color you want. As you move your cursor over various choices, a live display of the latest font color appears. You'll use green as an example.

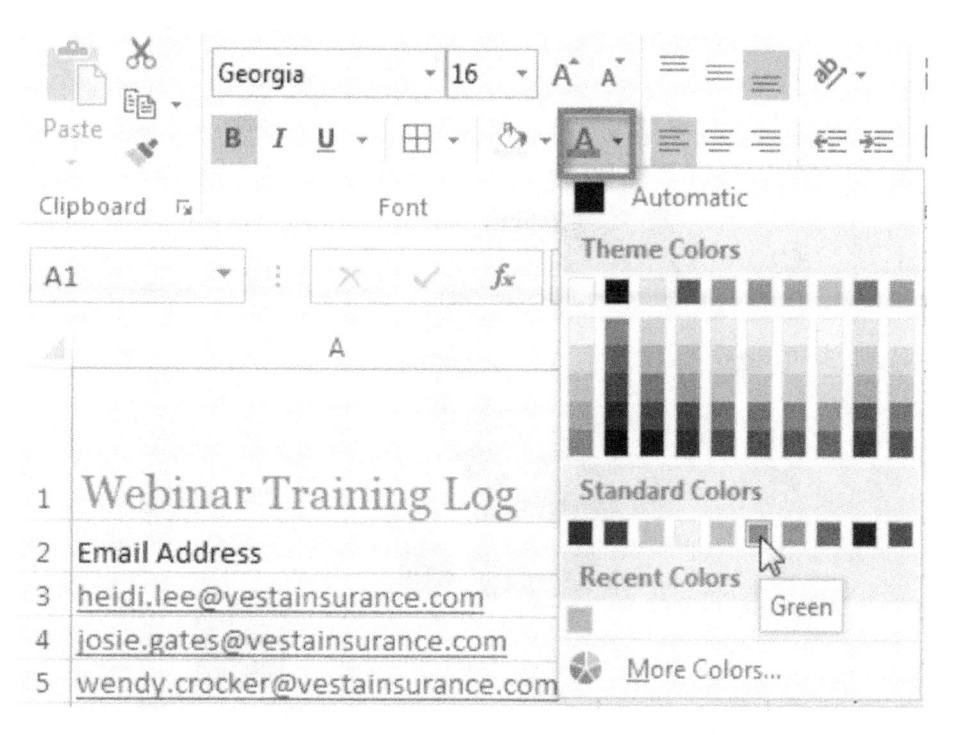

The font color you choose will be applied to the text.

10. To see more color choices, go to the bottom of the menu and choose "More Colors."

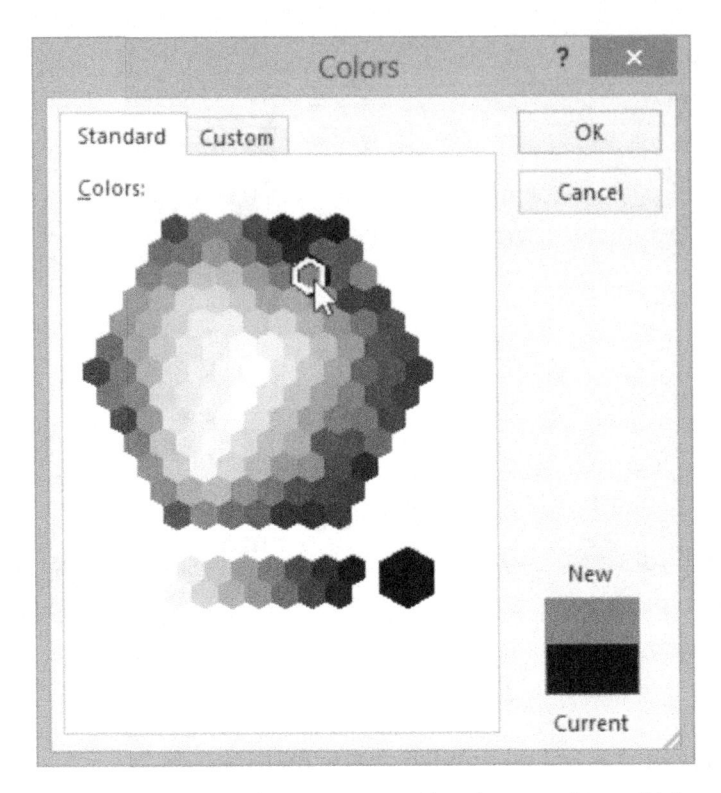

11. To utilize the Italic, Bold, and Underline commands, choose the cell(s) you would like to alter.

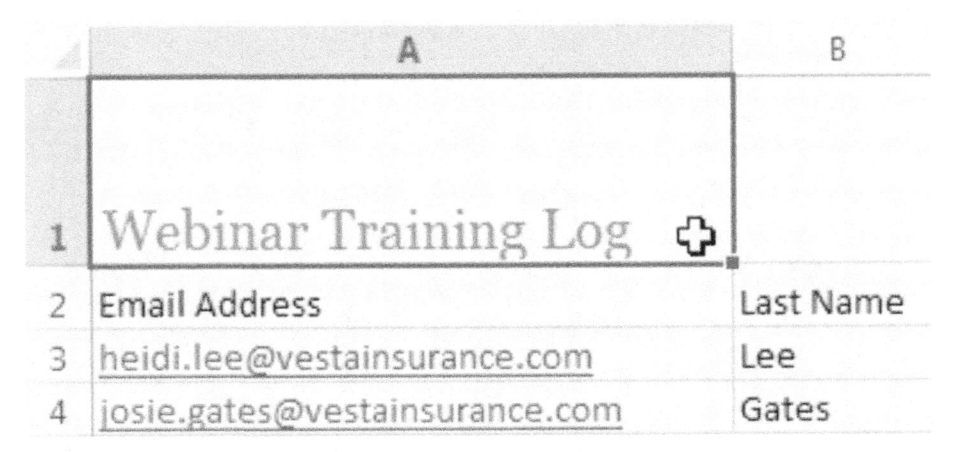

12. On the "Home" page, choose Bold (B), Underline (U), or Italic (I). You'll make a selected cell bold in this case.

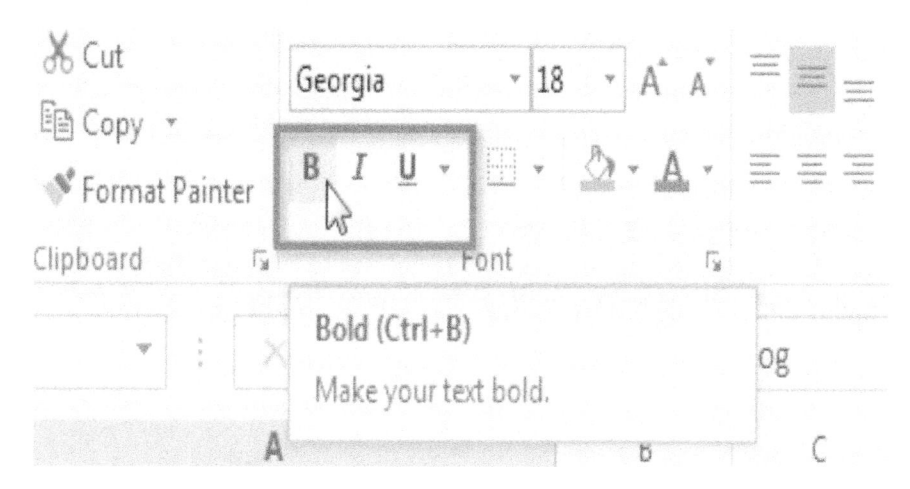

The text will be styled in the chosen format.

You can also make chosen text bold by pressing "Ctrl+B" on the screen, italic by pressing "Ctrl+I," and underline it by pressing "Ctrl+U."

Text Alignment

Text inserted into the worksheet is aligned at the bottom-left of the cell by default, while numbers are aligned at the bottom-right. Changing the orientation of the cell content helps you customize how well the content in each cell is viewed, making it easy to interpret.

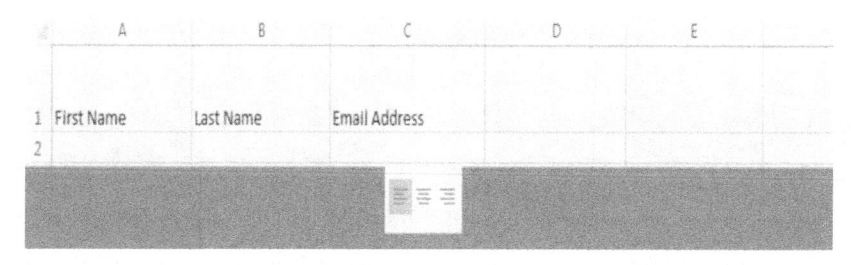

Left Align: This aligns text to the cell's left boundary.

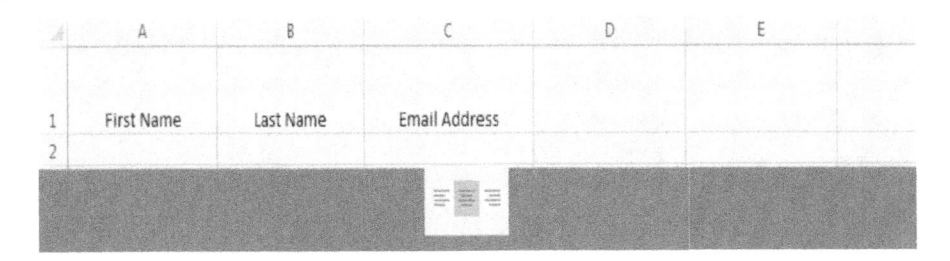

Center Align: This aligns data evenly between the cell's left and right boundaries.

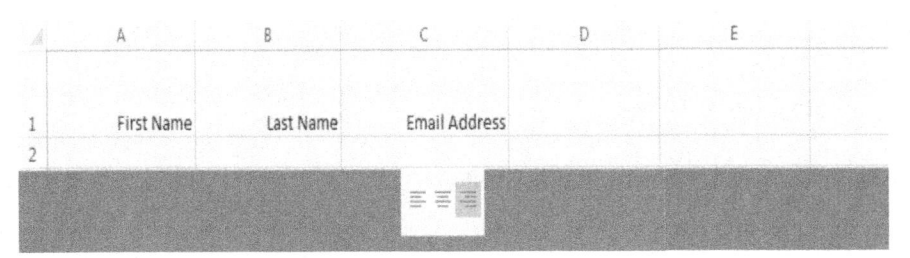

Right Align: This aligns the content to the cell's right border.

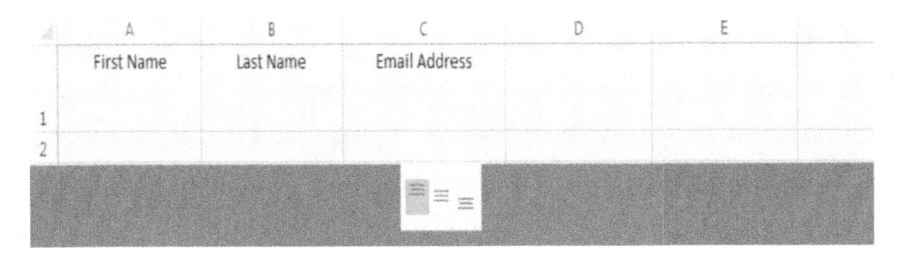

Top Align: This aligns the content to the cell's top border.

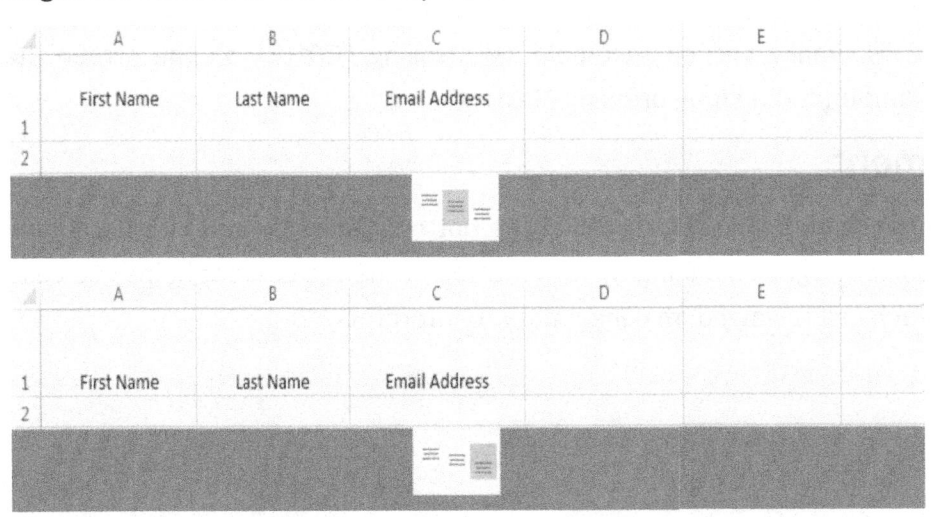

Middle Align: This aligns data at a constant distance from the cell's top and bottom edges.

Bottom Align: This aligns data to the cell's bottom border.

To modify horizontal text alignment, you'll change the orientation of the title cell in this example to give it a more finished appearance and set it apart from the remainder of your worksheet.

1. Choose the cell(s) you would like to alter.

2. On your "Home" tab, choose one of the three horizontal orientation commands. You'll use "Center Align" as an example here.

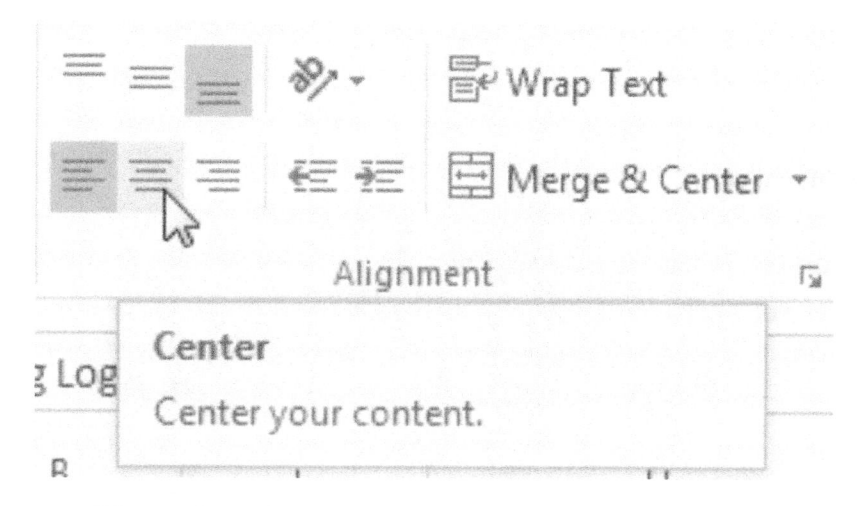

The document will be realigned.

3. To change vertical text alignment, choose the cell(s) you would like to alter.

4. On your "Home" page, choose one of the three vertical orientation commands. You'll use "Middle Align" in the following example.

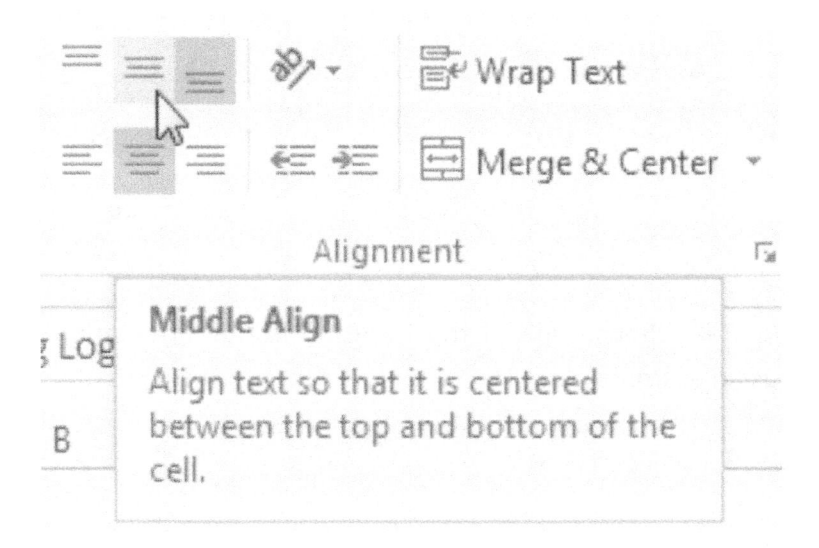

Middle Align
Align text so that it is centered between the top and bottom of the cell.

Your text then realigns.

Any cell can have both vertical and horizontal orientation settings applied to it.

Cell Borders and Fill Colors

You can build simple and established boundaries for various parts of the worksheet using cell borders and fill colors. To better separate the header cells from the rest of a worksheet, you can apply cell borders and fill them with color.

1. To add a border, choose the cell(s) you would like to alter.

2. On the "Home" page, click the drop-down arrow beside the "Borders" command. A drop-down menu for "Borders" will appear.

48 | EXCELL ACCELERATOR

3. Choose one border style for your document. You'll use the "All-Borders" option in the following case.

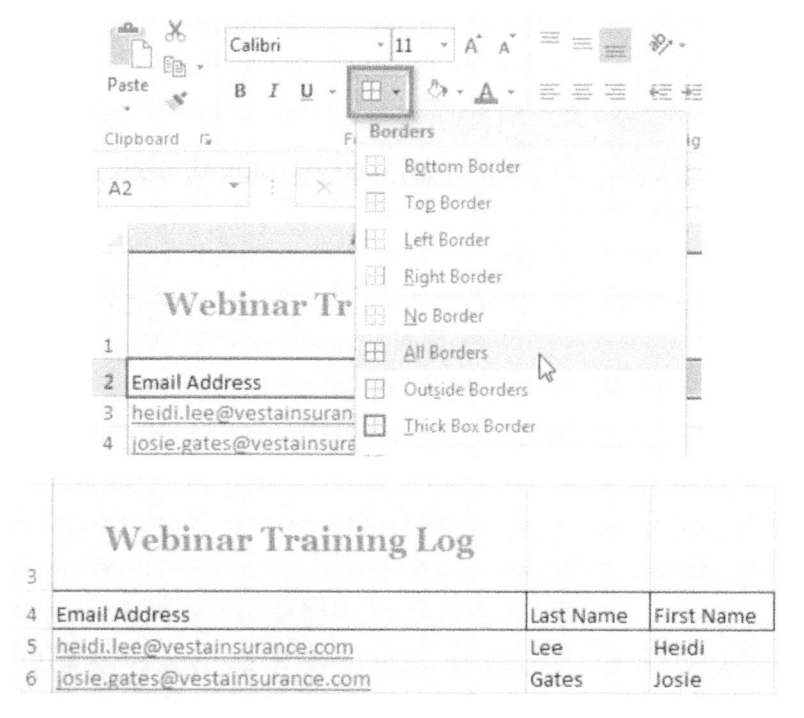

The chosen border style will be shown.

With the "Draw Borders" features at the base of Borders's drop-down menu, you can draw borders and adjust their line style and color.

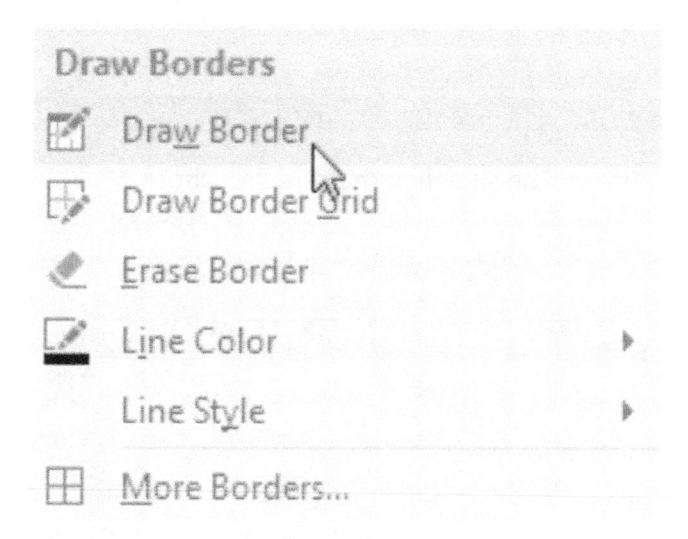

4. To add the fill color, choose the cell(s) you would like to alter.

5. On the "Home" page, click that drop-down arrow beside the "Fill Color" command. You'll see the "Fill-Color" menu displayed.
6. Choose the paint you intend to use for the fill. As you move your cursor over various choices, a live display of the latest fill color appears. You'll use "Light Green" in the following example:

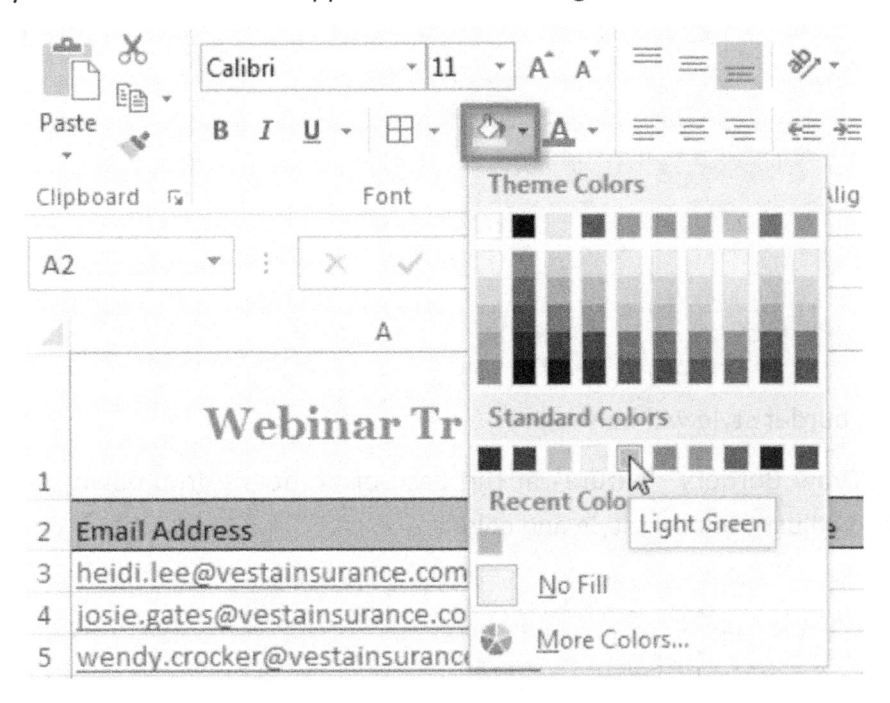

The fill color you choose will be shown in the cells you chose.

Format Painter

You can use the "Format Painter" function on your "Home" tab to copy formatting from one cell to another. Format Painter can copy all formatting from the chosen cell when you click it. The formatting can then be pasted on any cells by clicking and dragging across them.

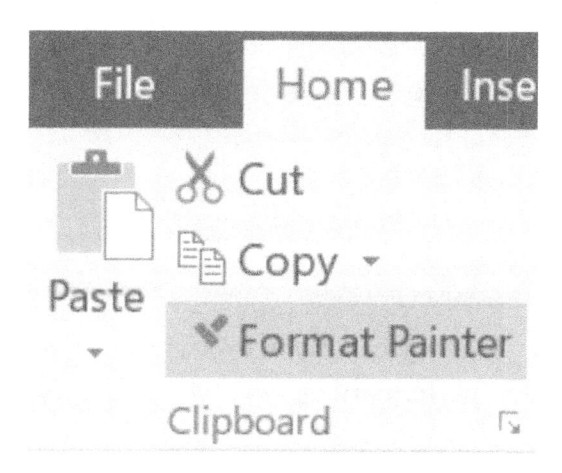

Cell Styles

You can use Excel's pre-designed cell styles instead of manually formatting cells. Cell styles have become an easy way to add skilled styling to sections of your workbook, including titles and headers.

To apply cell style, you'll add some new cell styles to your current title and header cells in the following case.

1. Choose the cell(s) you would like to alter.

2. Select the "Cell Styles" option on the "Home" tab, then select the desired style in your drop-down menu. You'll use Accent 1 in the following example.

The chosen cell style is shown.

	Webinar Training Log		
3			
4	Email Address	Last Name	First Name
5	heidi.lee@vestainsurance.com	Lee	Heidi
6	josie.gates@vestainsurance.com	Gates	Josie

Except for the text alignment, applying cell style overwrites all previous cell formatting. If your workbook already has a variety of formatting, you will probably not want to utilize cell-style formatting.

Formatting Text and Numbers

The opportunity to add complex formatting to text and numbers is among Excel's most important features. You can utilize formatting to adjust the appearance of days, hours, decimals, currencies ($), percentages (%), and many more, rather than showing all the cell material in the same format.

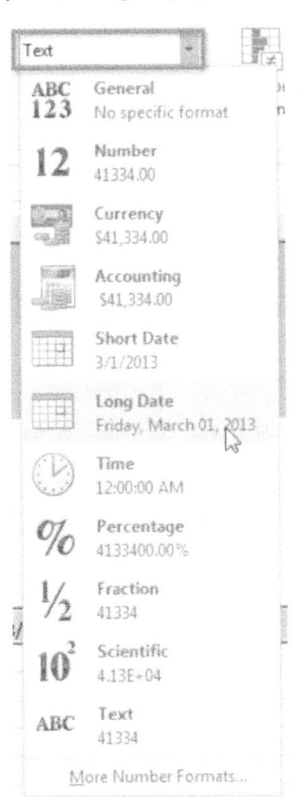

For applying number formatting, to adjust the way dates are presented, you'll change the number format for a range of cells in the following example.

1. Choose the cell(s) you would like to alter.

3/1/2013	3/8/2013	3/15/2013	3/22/2013	3/29/2013
X	X			

2. On the "Home" page, click the drop-down arrow beside the "Number Format" option. A drop-down menu for Number Formatting will appear.

3. Choose the formatting alternative you want. You'll adjust the formatting for "Long Date" in the following example.

The newest formatting style will be applied to the chosen cells. You can adjust the numbers of decimal places shown in certain number formats by using the "Increase Decimal" and "Decrease Decimal" commands (underneath the "Number Format" option).

Friday, March 01, 2013 Friday, March 08, 2013 Friday, March 15, 2013 Friday, March 22, 2013 Friday, March 29, 2013
X   X

4. To familiarize yourself with the various number and text formatting options, use the buttons in the illustration below.

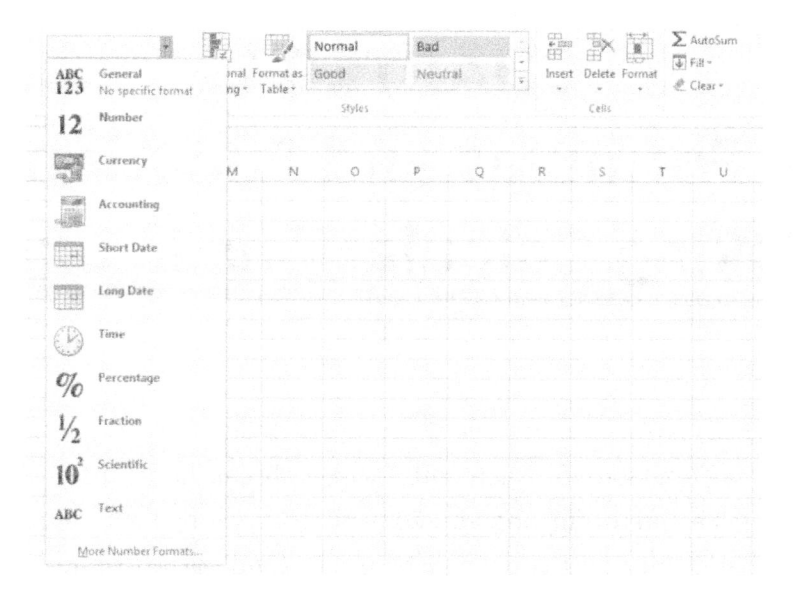

CHAPTER 2:
Basic Formulas and Functions and Making Calculations in Excel

Every formula, as well as functions of Microsoft Excel, is bread and butter. For both, you will feel everything more impressive and useful, and you will also enjoy doing something in a spreadsheet. This chapter presents the basic principles you need to understand to be confident while utilizing these formulas in Microsoft Excel.

How You Should Enter Formulas in Excel

Microsoft Excel utilizes the standard operators specifically for equations, i.e., a plus sign for sum (+), the minus sign for negation (-), the asterisk sign for multiplication (*), front slashing for division (/), and the caret (^) for exponents. There is the main point: In writing Microsoft Excel formulas, you must begin formulas with an equal symbol (=). This is necessary because the cell includes, or is equivalent to, the formula and its value.

Creating a Simple Formula Example in Excel

1. Choose the cell at which the answer appears (B4, shown example).

	A	B	C
1	Estimated painting cost per square foot		
2	Total cost	$75.00	
3	Square Feet	250	
4	Total/Sq Ft		
5			

2. Type a symbol equivalent (=).
3. Type the formula that you want Microsoft Excel to calculate (e.g., 75/250).

	A	B	C
	MAX	fx =75/250	
1	Estimated painting cost per square foot		
2	Total cost	$75.00	
3	Square Feet	250	
4	Total/Sq Ft	=75/250	
5			

4. By Pressing "Enter," the specific formula will finish the calculation, and the result will be seen in the said cell.

	A	B	C
	B4	fx =75/250	
1	Estimated painting cost per square foot		
2	Total cost	$75.00	
3	Square Feet	250	
4	Total/Sq Ft	$0.30	
5			

When the figures of a result of the formula are big in a cell, and it appears as a hash (#) rather than a value, it indicates that the columns are not large enough to show the cell's value. Now you have to manually increase the column's width to show the contents of the cells.

Creating the Formulas that Refer to the Other Cell inside the Same Worksheet

The reference of a cell address is always a variation of some column's letter and a row number that classify a cell in a worksheet. During the creation of cell reference at a similar sheet, the following points must be considered:

1. First, select the cell where you want to insert the formula. Now type the symbol "="
2. Now you want to type the accurate reference in the said cell or in the top bar called formula bar.
3. Select the appropriate cell to which you wish to refer.
4. Type the remaining formula and then press "Enter" for finishing.
5. For example, for adding the value in cells A1 and A2, you must type the "=" sign and click A1. Type the "+" sign, click A2, and then press "Enter."

	A	B	C
1	5		=A1+A2
2	10		

Click the cell to make a cell reference

6. If you want to make a range reference in Microsoft Excel, select the required cells on a specific worksheet.

7. For example, for adding the different values in cells A1, A2, or A3, then type the equal symbol followed up with the "SUM" method and the starting parenthesis. Select the cells with A1 to A3, and type the ending parenthesis, now press "Enter."

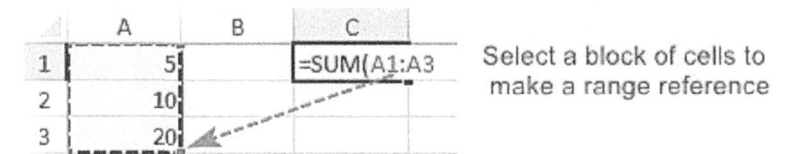

8. For granting the reference of the complete row or complete column, tap on the row number; otherwise, refer to the column letter.

9. For example, to merge all cells in a single row, start to type the "SUM" method. Now click the first Header of a row to indulge the reference row within your formula.

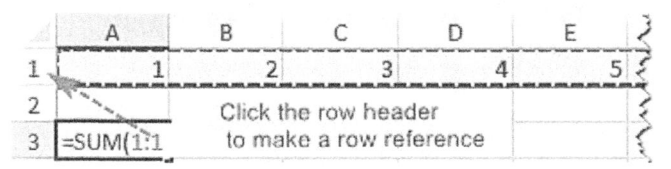

Create a Formula that Links to the Other Workbooks

Making links or other external cell references may be used to avoid the same data in different sheets—which saves time, decreases error, and increases data integrity. Conduct the following measures to make an external reference:

1. First, open all the workbooks.
2. Select the workbook named "Company" and choose cell B2, then type the equal symbol. 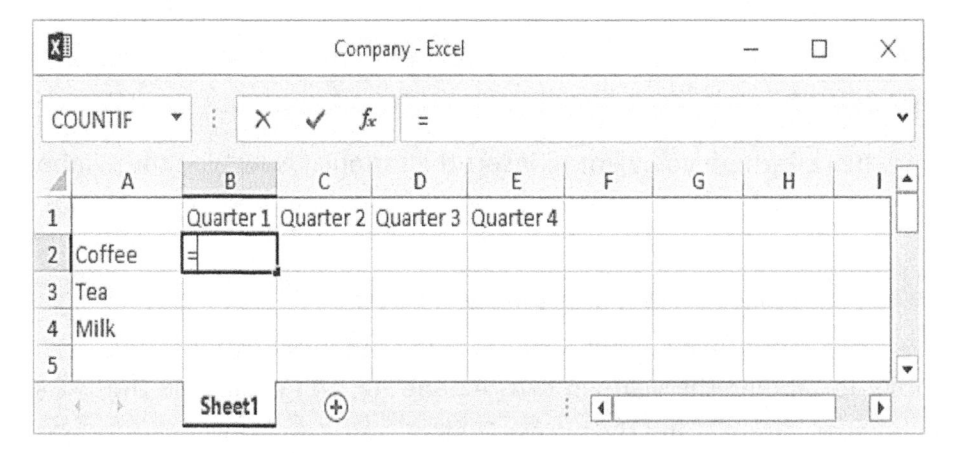
3. At the "View" tab, on the window group, select "Switch" windows.

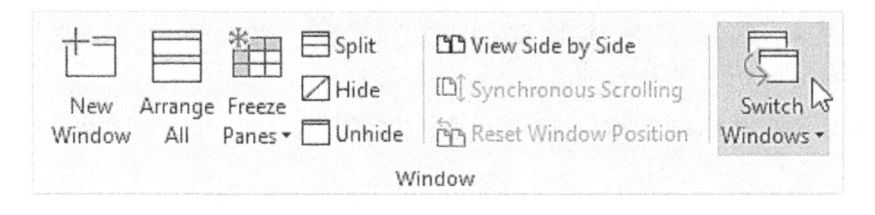

56 | EXCELL ACCELERATOR

4. Now click the workbook "North."
5. Pick cell B2 in the said workbook.

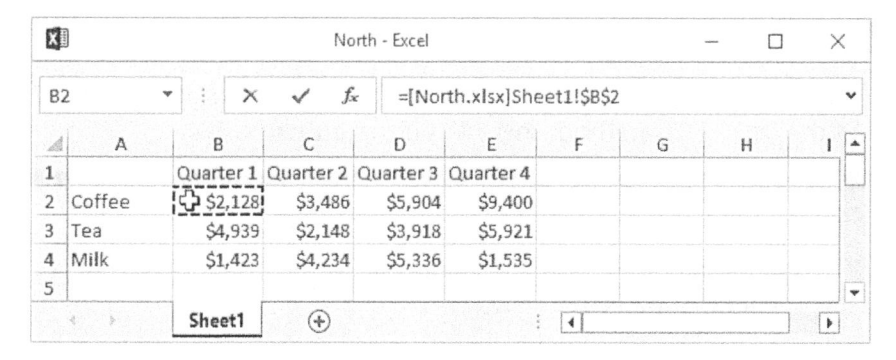

6. Now type the "+" sign.
7. Then repeat the steps from 3 to 6 for your "Mid" workbook.
8. Repeat the steps from 3 to 5 for your "South" workbook.
9. Finally, delete the "$" signs in the cell B2 formula for further proceeding.

Results:

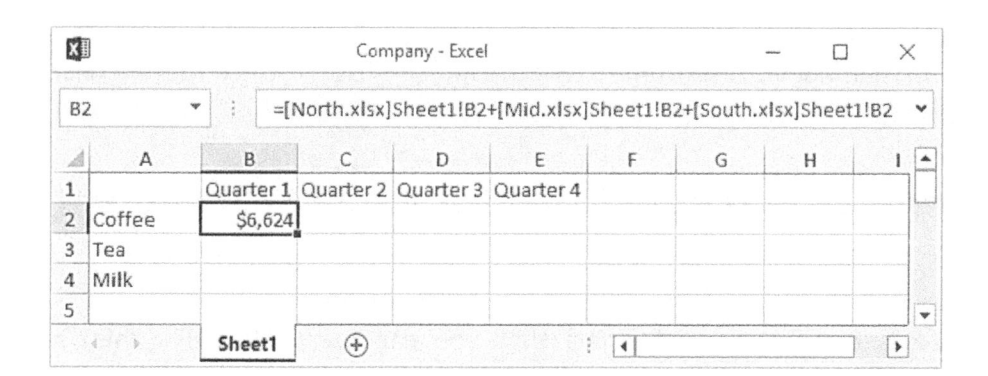

Use of Apostrophes for Enclosing and to Full the File Name and the Worksheet Name

By using the "INDIRECT" method of Excel, you can change a text string for correct reference. You may utilize the "&" operator to make a text series. Take a look at the "INDIRECT" method mentioned below:

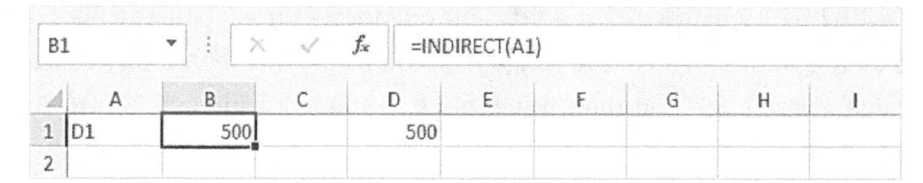

"=INDIRECT (A1)" is shortened to "=INDIRECT ("D1")" and the INDIRECT method change the text string "D1" as a correct cell reference, and in other terms, "=INDIRECT ("D1")" is shortened to =D1.

The basic INDIRECT function mentioned below achieves almost a similar result.

	A	B	C	D	E	F	G	H	I
B1		fx	=INDIRECT("D1")						
1		500		500					
2									

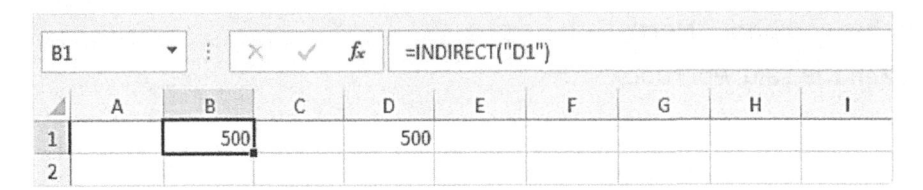

Without the usage of the INDIRECT method, this will be the outcome.

	A	B	C	D	E	F	G	H	I
B1		fx	=A1						
1	D1	D1		500					
2									

The use of the "&" operator links the "D" string along with the value in cell A1.

	A	B	C	D	E	F	G	H	I
B1		fx	=INDIRECT("D"&A1)						
1	1	500		500					
2									

The formula mentioned above is shortened to "=INDIRECT ("D1")." Once more, "=INDIRECT ("D1")" is shortened to "=D1."

Basic Formulas and Functions for Excel Workflow

SUM

The SUM feature is the first Excel formula that you can learn. It is like this "=SUM (number1, [number2], …)."

The formula "=SUM(A10:A12)" will add up all the values given in the range, starting from Cell A10 and ending at A12.

The formula "=SUM(B2:G2)" will add up all the values given in the range, starting from Cell B2 and ending at G8.

The formula "=SUM(B2:B7,B9,B12:B15)" is a little bit advance as it will start to function in such a way that it will add up all the values given in the range from B2 to B7. It will omit any value in cell B8, then it will add up the value given in B9, and then it will omit all the values in cell B10 to B11 and add up all the values of B12 to B15.

"=SUM(A2:A8)" using this given formula and dividing it by 20 will give you a result in which you can turn your fraction into a simple formula.

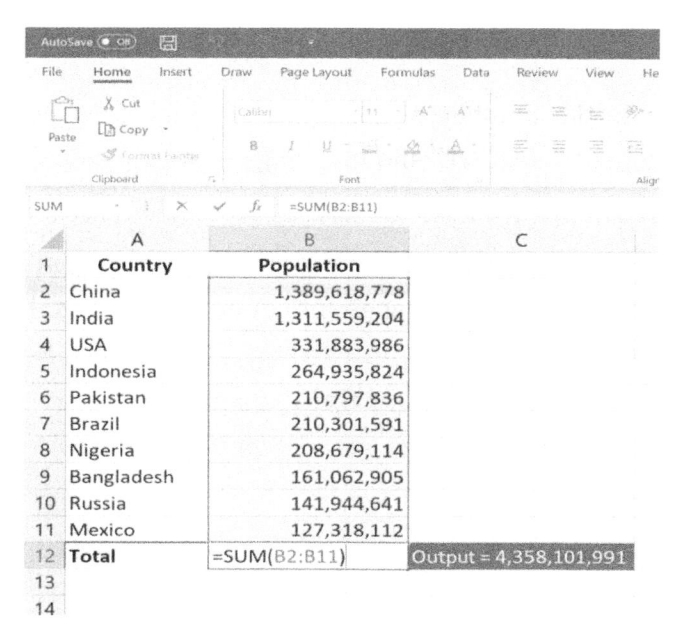

	A	B	C
1	Country	Population	
2	China	1,389,618,778	
3	India	1,311,559,204	
4	USA	331,883,986	
5	Indonesia	264,935,824	
6	Pakistan	210,797,836	
7	Brazil	210,301,591	
8	Nigeria	208,679,114	
9	Bangladesh	161,062,905	
10	Russia	141,944,641	
11	Mexico	127,318,112	
12	Total	=SUM(B2:B11)	Output = 4,358,101,991

The Use of "AVERAGE"

This function helps in finding out the simple averages for a given set of data; for example, you can easily calculate the average results of the stockholder in a shareholding pool; to do that, you can use the given formula.

"=AVERAGE" followed by this syntax, which includes (number 1,2,3 and so on…)."

The formula "=AVERAGE(B4:B12)" will result in an average value of a range starting from B4 and ending at B12.

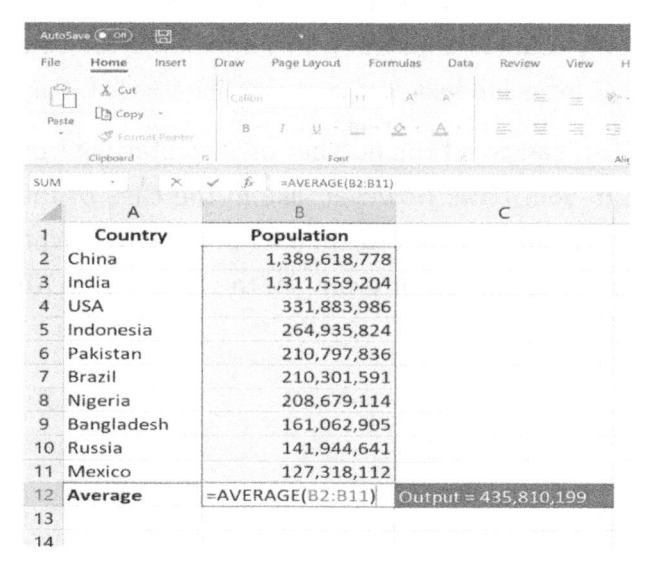

	A	B	C
1	Country	Population	
2	China	1,389,618,778	
3	India	1,311,559,204	
4	USA	331,883,986	
5	Indonesia	264,935,824	
6	Pakistan	210,797,836	
7	Brazil	210,301,591	
8	Nigeria	208,679,114	
9	Bangladesh	161,062,905	
10	Russia	141,944,641	
11	Mexico	127,318,112	
12	Average	=AVERAGE(B2:B11)	Output = 435,810,199

COUNT

The "COUNT" feature counts the number of cells in a set that only includes numeric values. For example, the formula given here "=COUNT" and inserting "(value1,[value2]...)" will count the numeric values.

The function "COUNT (A:A)" will help you count all the given values in a set that are numerical and are lying at "A." You are required to modify the range for counting the rows. For example, "COUNT" and insert "(A1:C1)" to count rows.

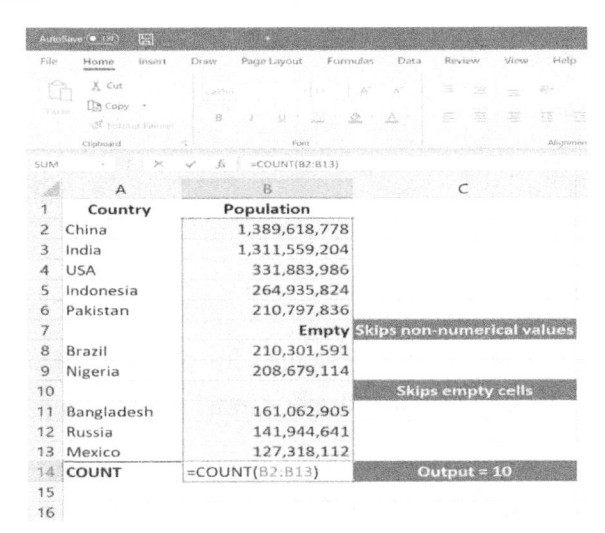

COUNTA

"COUNTA," like the "COUNT" feature, counts all cells in a rage. It does, however, egardless of their kind. Unlike COUNT, which only counts numerically, this function often counts days, hours, sequences, logical values, mistakes, null strings, and text. The syntax is like this "=COUNTA (value1, [value2], …)."

The formula "COUNTA(C2:C13)" can count the number of rows starting from 2 to 13 inside column C—no matter what is the type of your data. However, like in the case of the "COUNT" function, a user can't use the same or exact formula for counting the number of rows. While using this formula, a user must adjust the range inside the brackets; for example, the formula "COUNTA(C2:H2)" will result in a total count of values from column C to H.

count all cells r

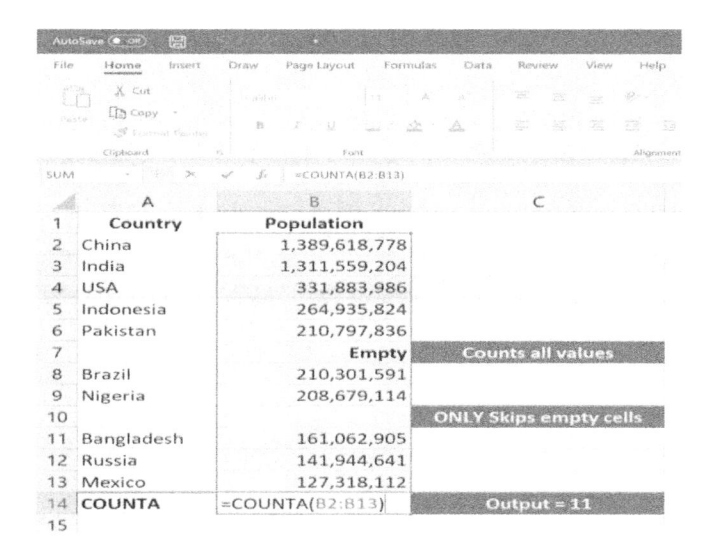

IF

When you choose to sort the data according to a set of rules, the "IF" feature is often used. The nice thing about the "IF" formula is that it allows you to use formulas and functions.

For example, the syntax "=IF" followed by any logical test, then true or false if the value is true, the result will be true otherwise false.

For example, the function "=IF (J2<K3, "TRUE" else "FALSE")" will test if any value given in the cell K3 is greater than the cell value at J2. The results will be true or false depending upon the logic of the function.

An example to understand this complicated "IF" logic can be: "=IF(B2>C2,True,False)." This function will check if any value given in cell B2 is greater than the cell value of C2. It will show "True" in the column where the formula is being typed; otherwise, it will result in "False" value in the cell.

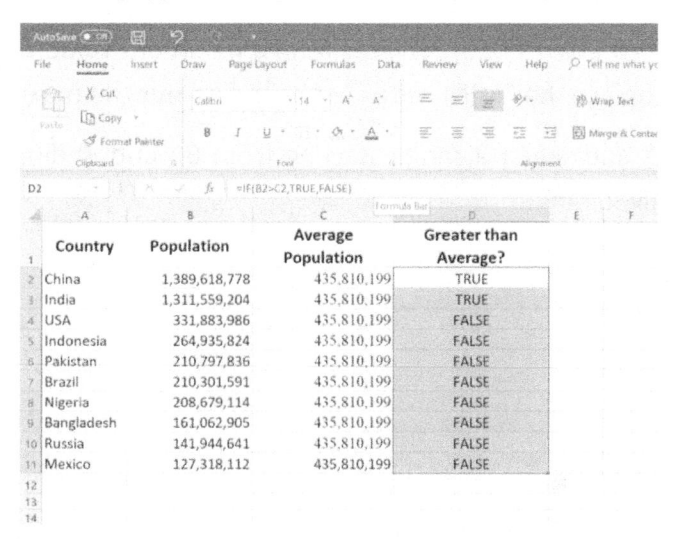

61 | EXCELL ACCELERATOR

TRIM

The "TRIM" function ensures that unruly spaces do not cause errors in your functions. It means that there are no vacant spaces. "TRIM" only works on a single cell—unlike other functions that may work on a group of cells. As a result, it has the drawback of duplicating details in a spreadsheet. The syntax is "=TRIM (text)." For example, "TRIM(A2)" eliminates the empty places in the cell A2 value.

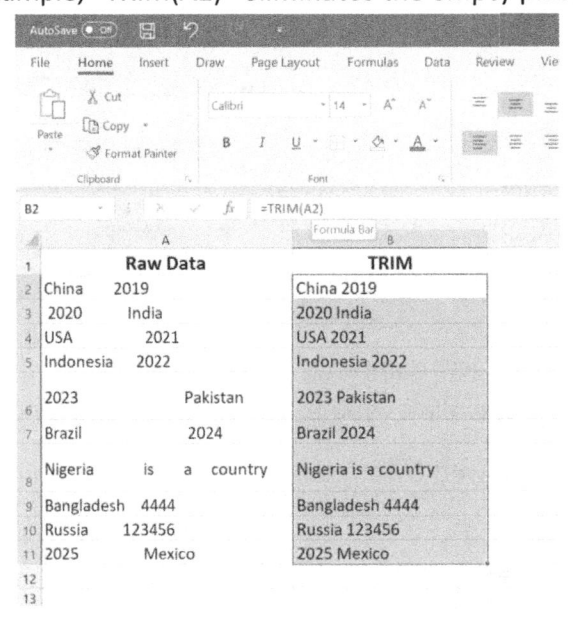

MAX and MIN

The functions "Max" and "MIN" are normally used to find out the greatest and smallest values in a given set. The function will be as follows.

First of all, type the "=" sign and then enter "MIN" or "Max." Then select a number or a range.

For example, the formula "=MIN(C15:C20)" will result in a minimum value residing in the range of C15 to C20. Similarly, you can replace the "MIN" with "MAX" to find out the maximum value.

For example, type "=MAX" and select a range starting from B2 and ending at C11, and it will find a maximum number in this given range.

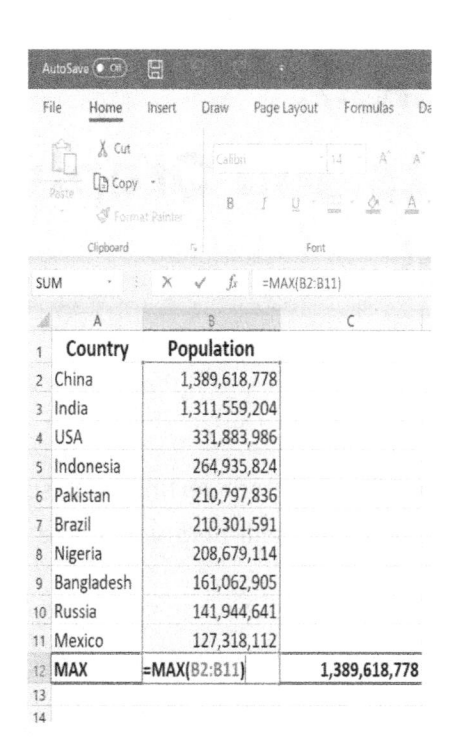

	A	B	C
1	Country	Population	
2	China	1,389,618,778	
3	India	1,311,559,204	
4	USA	331,883,986	
5	Indonesia	264,935,824	
6	Pakistan	210,797,836	
7	Brazil	210,301,591	
8	Nigeria	208,679,114	
9	Bangladesh	161,062,905	
10	Russia	141,944,641	
11	Mexico	127,318,112	
12	MAX	=MAX(B2:B11)	1,389,618,778

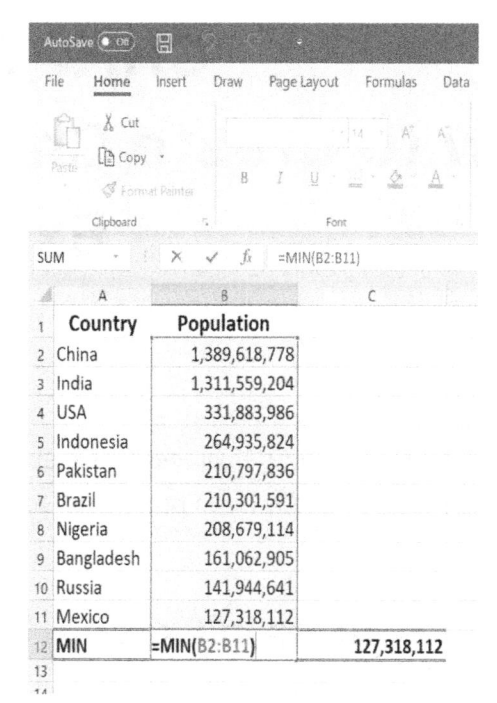

	A	B	C
1	Country	Population	
2	China	1,389,618,778	
3	India	1,311,559,204	
4	USA	331,883,986	
5	Indonesia	264,935,824	
6	Pakistan	210,797,836	
7	Brazil	210,301,591	
8	Nigeria	208,679,114	
9	Bangladesh	161,062,905	
10	Russia	141,944,641	
11	Mexico	127,318,112	
12	MIN	=MIN(B2:B11)	127,318,112

CHAPTER 3:
How to Create Charts and Graphs in Excel

Excel is used to store data in all businesses. Excel will assist you in converting your spreadsheet data into charts and graphs to get a clear picture of your data, and it will help you make better business decisions.

Graphs and Charts in Excel

Excel makes it simple to make graphs and charts, particularly when you can save your data in an Excel Workbook instead of importing it from another program. Excel also has a number of pre-designed graph and chart types from which you can choose the one that best represents the data relationships you want to emphasize.

Forms and Types of Charts

Excel has a large chart and graph library to help you visually display your results. You can, of course, add graphical elements to a chart or graph to improve and customize it. The following are major types of charts or graphs in Excel 2016:

Column Charts

Column charts are ideal for comparing data or when there are multiple categories within a single variable. There are seven different column chart categories available in Excel: 3-D stacked, 3-D clustered, clustered, 100% stacked, 3-D stacked, and 3-D 100% stacked, pictured below. Choose the visual representation that best plots your data.

Bar Charts

Bar charts differ from column charts in that the bars are horizontal rather than vertical. Although you can use bar charts and column charts interchangeably, some people prefer column charts when dealing with negative values because it's easier to represent negatives vertically on the y-axis.

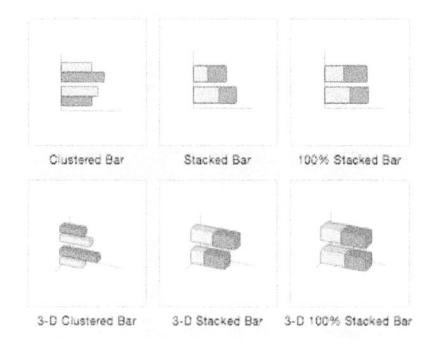

Line Charts

A line chart is best for displaying trends over time instead of static data points. Each data point is connected by a line, allowing you to see how the values have changed over time. The line chart options are stacked line, line, line with markers, 100% stacked line, 3-D line, stacked line with markers, and 100% stacked line with markers.

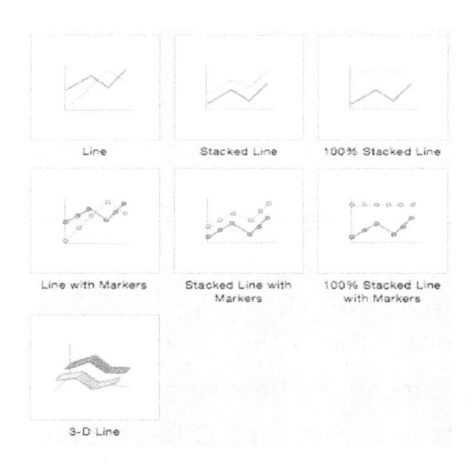

Pie Charts

Use pie charts to compare the proportions of a whole (the sum of your data's values). Each value is displayed by a pie piece, allowing you to see the proportions. There are five types of pie charts: Pie, bar of pie, pie of pie (which divides 1 pie into 2 to indicate sub-category proportions), doughnut, and 3-D pie.

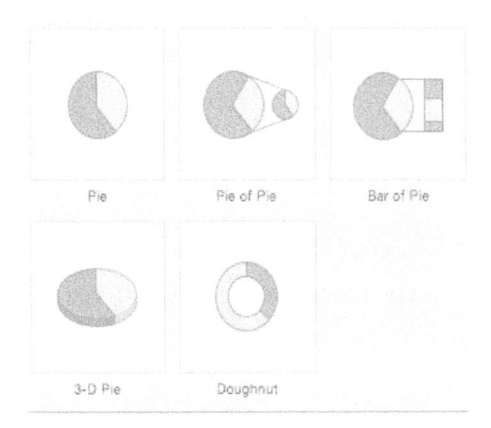

Scatter Charts

Scatter charts are used to display how one variable influences another. They are similar to line graphs in that they are useful for displaying changes in variables over time. (This is referred to as correlation.) Bubble charts, which are a common chart form, are classified as scatter. These are the scatter chart options: Scatter with straight lines and markers, scatter with smooth lines and markers, scatter, scatter with straight lines, scatter with smooth lines, 3-D bubble, and bubble.

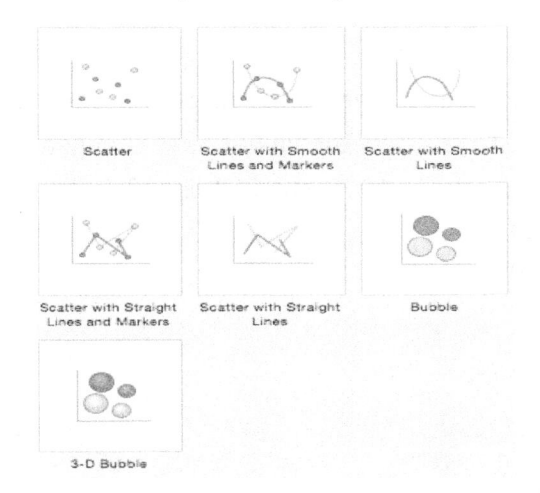

Area

Area charts, like line charts, represent the change in values over time. Area charts are useful for highlighting differences in change among multiple variables because the area beneath each line is solid. There are six area charts: Stacked area, area, 3-D area, 100% stacked area, 3-D 100% stacked area, and 3-D stacked area.

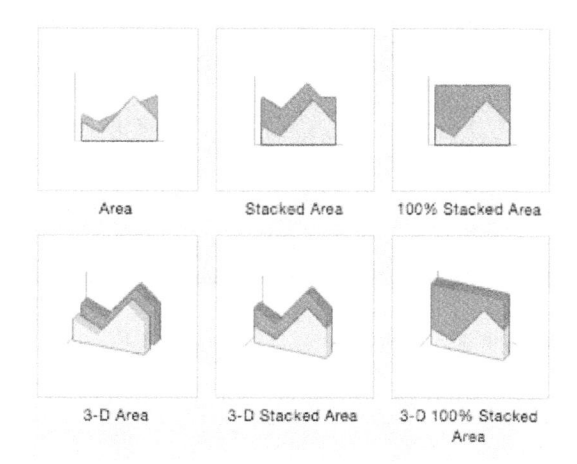

Stock

This form of chart is used in financial analysis and by investors to show the high, low, and closing price of a stock. However, if you want to show the range of a value (or the range of its expected value) and its exact value, you can use them in any case. Stock chart options are: open-high-low-close, volume-open-high-low-close, high-low-close, and volume-high-low-close.

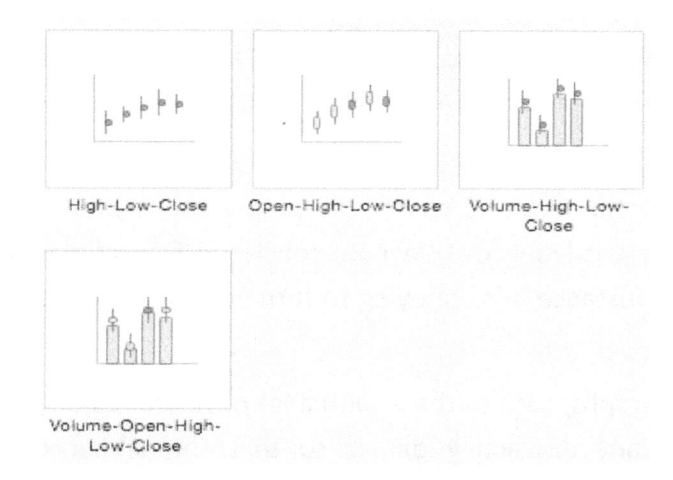

Surface

To represent data over a 3-D landscape, use a surface chart. Large data sets, data sets with more than 2 variables, and data sets with groups within a single variable benefit from this additional plane. However, surface maps can be difficult to understand, so make sure the audience knows what they're looking at. You can select from contour, 3-D surface, wireframe contour, and wireframe 3-D surface.

3-D Surface   Wireframe 3-D Surface   Contour

Wireframe Contour

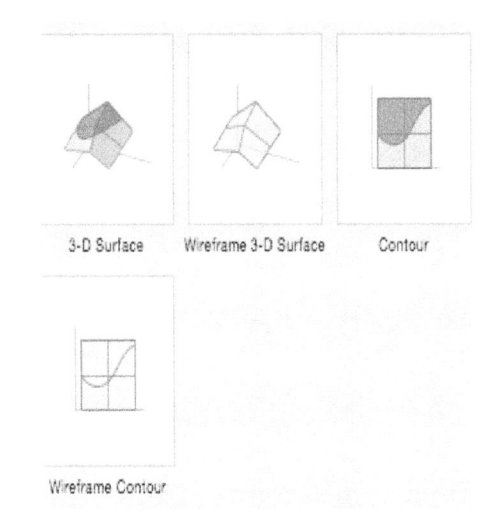

Best Ways to Create a Chart and Graph

While Excel has many layout and formatting presets to help you improve the look and readability of your chart, using them will not guarantee that your chart will be as effective as it could be. Here are the best ways to make your chart or graph as clear and functional as possible:

Choose Suitable Themes: When choosing a theme, think about your audience, the subject, and the chart's main point. While experimenting with various styles can be fun, select a theme that best fits your requirements.

Use Text Carefully: Despite the fact that charts and graphs are mostly visual tools, you can almost certainly have text (such as axis labels or titles). Be concise but descriptive and be careful about the orientation of any text (for instance, it's annoying to turn your head to view text written sideways on the x-axis).

Make It Simple: Cluttered graphs, such as those with a lot of text or colors, are hard to read and don't attract the eye. Remove any distracting details so that the audience can concentrate on the information you are presenting.

Place Elements Wisely: Pay close attention to where symbols, titles, graphical elements, and legends are placed. They should support your chart rather than distract you from it.

Sort Data Before Creating the Chart: When people forget to sort their data or delete duplicates before making a chart, the visual becomes unintuitive and may lead to errors.

How to Make Chart Data in Excel

1. You must first provide Excel with data from which to create a chart or graph.
2. Enter data into a worksheet.
3. Select "New Workbook" from the "File" menu in Excel.

4. To create a chart or graph, enter the data you want to use. We're comparing the profit of five different items from 2013 to 2017 in this example. Make sure that your columns and rows have labels. As a result, you'll be able to convert the data into a graph or chart with specific axis labels.

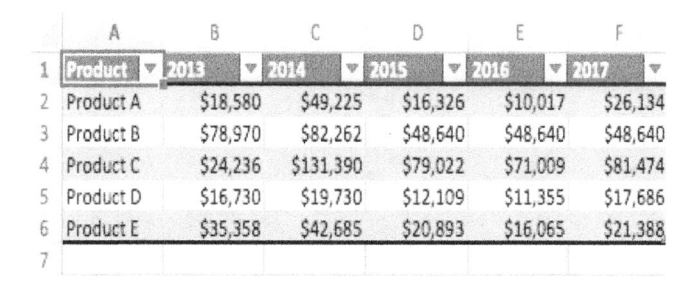

Product	2013	2014	2015	2016	2017
Product A	$18,580	$49,225	$16,326	$10,017	$26,134
Product B	$78,970	$82,262	$48,640	$48,640	$48,640
Product C	$24,236	$131,390	$79,022	$71,009	$81,474
Product D	$16,730	$19,730	$12,109	$11,355	$17,686
Product E	$35,358	$42,685	$20,893	$16,065	$21,388

5. Choose "Range" to make a graph or chart from workbook data.
6. By dragging your mouse over the cells, you can highlight the cells that contain the data you want to use in your graph.
7. You can now choose a chart style after your cell range has been outlined in gray.

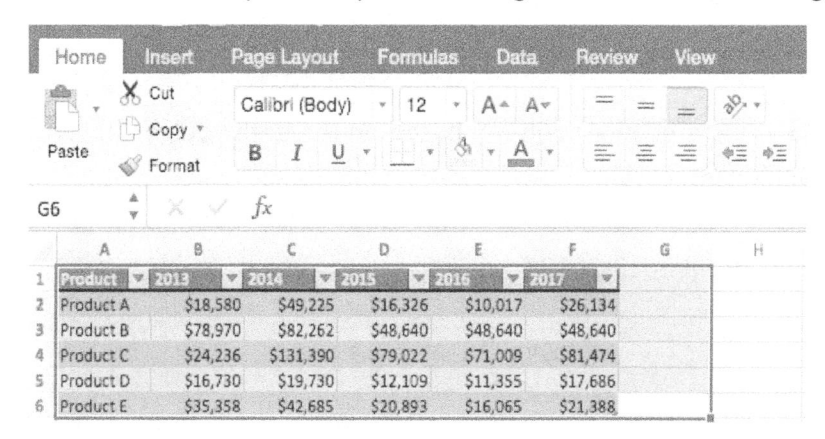

We'll go over how to make a clustered column chart in Excel in the following segment.

How to Make a Chart in Excel

After you've entered your data and selected a cell range, you'll have to select a chart type to display it.

Step 1: Choose Chart Type

A segment with many chart options is located about halfway across the toolbar. Excel provides suggested charts based on popularity, but you can choose a different design by clicking any of the dropdown menus.

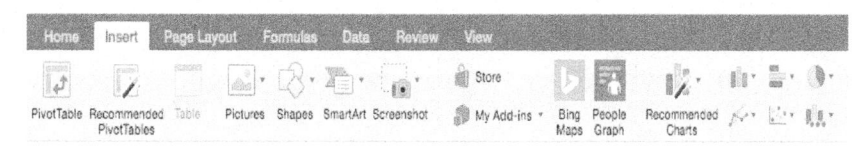

69 | EXCELL ACCELERATOR

Step 2: Make Your Chart

1. Select "Clustered Column" from the "Column Chart" icon on the "Insert" tab.

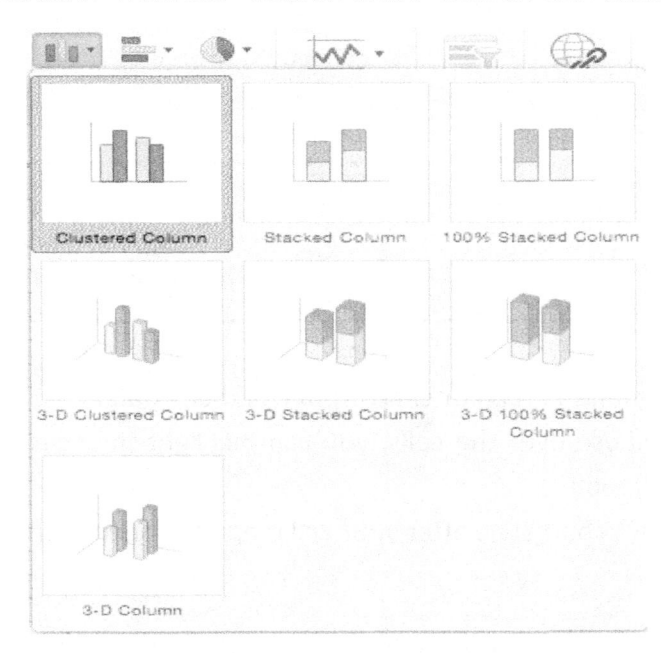

2. Excel will build a clustered chart column based on the data you've chosen. The chart will appear in the workbook's center.
3. To give your chart a name, double-click the "Chart Title" text and enter a title. We will title this chart as "Product Profit 2013-2017."

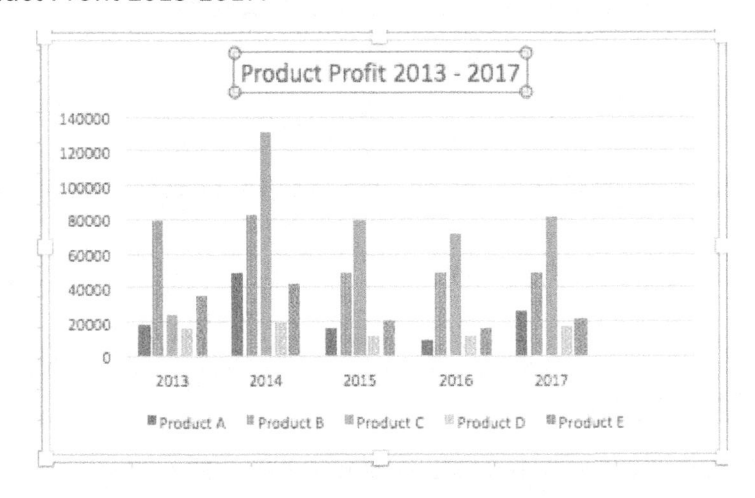

COLUMN CHART TEMPLATE

PRODUCT	2013	2014	2015	2016	2017
Product A	$18,580	$49,225	$16,326	$10,017	$26,134
Product B	$78,970	$82,262	$48,640	$48,640	$48,640
Product C	$24,236	$131,390	$79,022	$71,009	$81,474
Product D	$16,730	$19,730	$12,109	$11,355	$17,686
Product E	$35,358	$42,685	$20,893	$16,065	$21,388

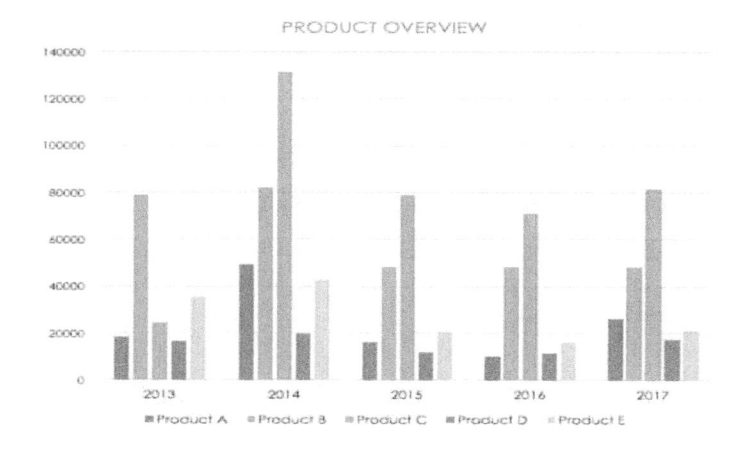

You can use the two tabs on the toolbar, "Chart Design" and "Format," to make adjustments to your chart.

Step 3: Add Chart Elements

Introducing chart elements to your graph or chart will modify it by including context or simplifying data. While using the "Add Chart Element" dropdown menu in the upper left section (below the "Home" tab), you can choose a chart element.

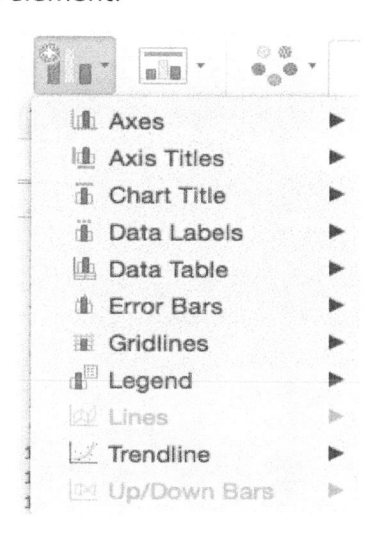

- Axes
- Axis Titles
- Chart Title
- Data Labels
- Data Table
- Error Bars
- Gridlines
- Legend
- Lines
- Trendline
- Up/Down Bars

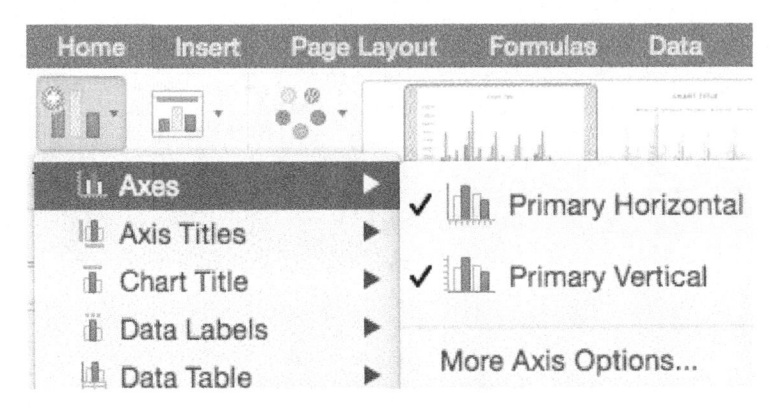

1. To make your chart's display axis disappear, uncheck these options.

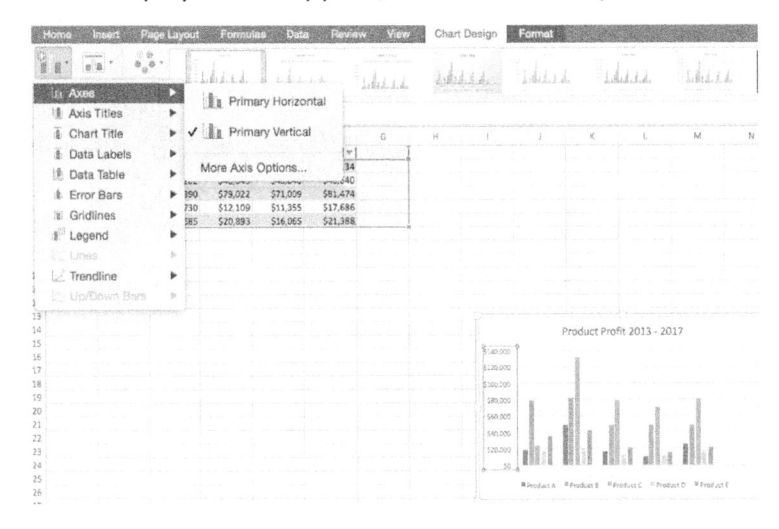

2.

From the "Axes" dropdown menu, select "More Axis Option" to open a window with additional text and formatting options, such as adding labels, tick marks or numbers, or changing text size and color.

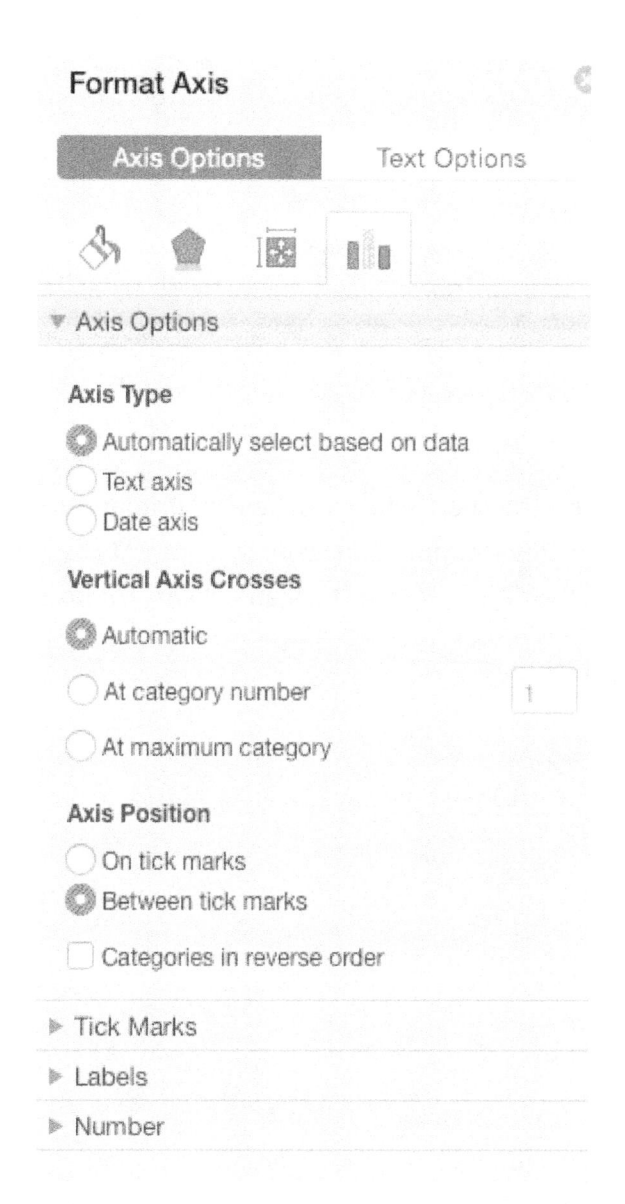

To Add Axis Titles:

1. Choose "Axis Titles" from the drop-down menu of "Add Chart Element." Since Axis Titles are not automatically added to charts in Excel, both "Primary Horizontal" and "Primary Vertical" will be unmarked.

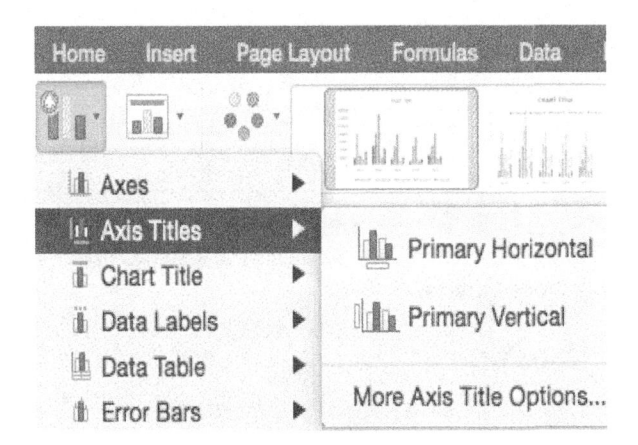

A text box will display on the chart when you select "Primary Horizontal" or "Primary Vertical" to create axis titles. In this example, we selected both. Type the titles to your axis. In this example, we give the titles "Profit" for vertical and "Year" for horizontal.

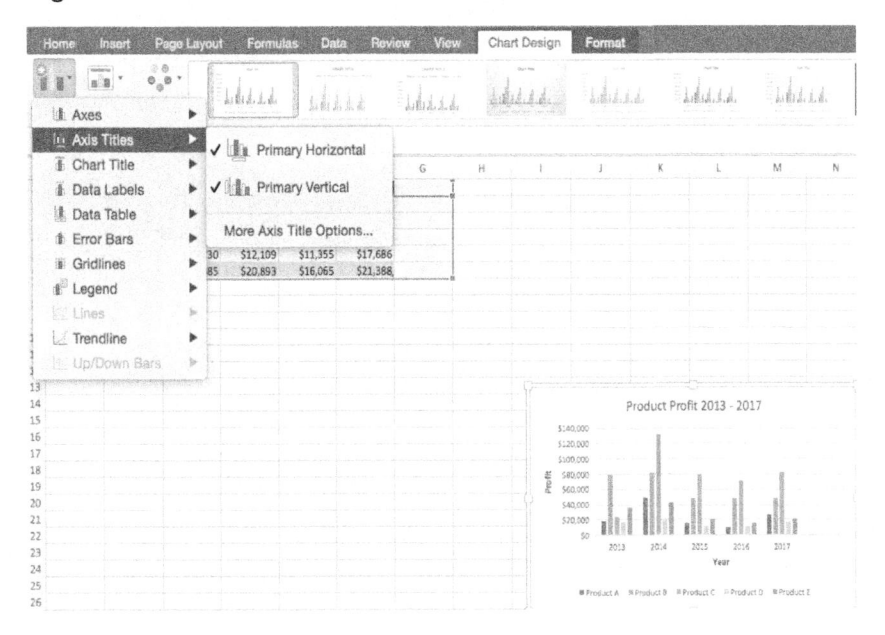

To Remove or Move the Chart Title:

1. Select "Chart Title" from the "Add Chart Element" drop-down menu ("Above Chart," "None," "Centered Overlay," and "More"). "Title Choices" are the 4 options you'll see.

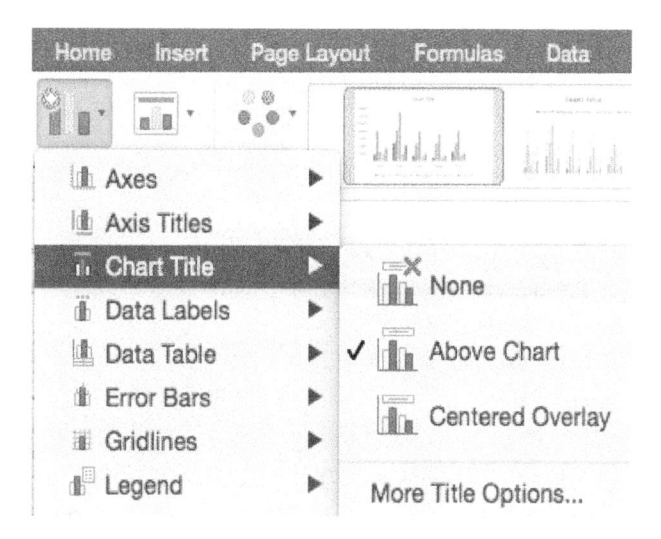

To Place the Title above the Chart:

1. Click "Above Chart." When you create a chart title, Excel will automatically set it above the chart.
2. Click none to remove the chart title.

To Place the Title inside the Chart's Gridlines:

1. Choose "Centered Overlay." Use this option carefully; you don't want the title to hide your data or clutter up your graph.

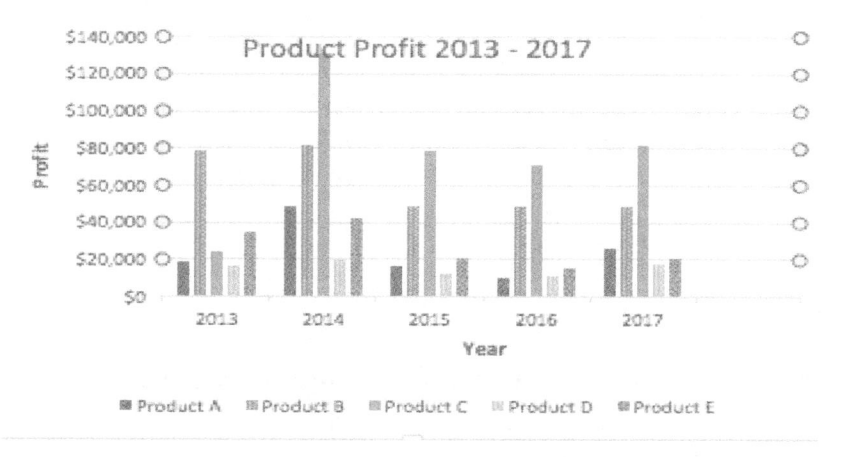

To Add Data Labels:

1. Select "Data Labels" from the "Add Chart Element" menu. For data labels, there are 6 options: "Center," "Inside End," "None" (default), "Outside End," "Inside Base," and "More Data Label Title Options."

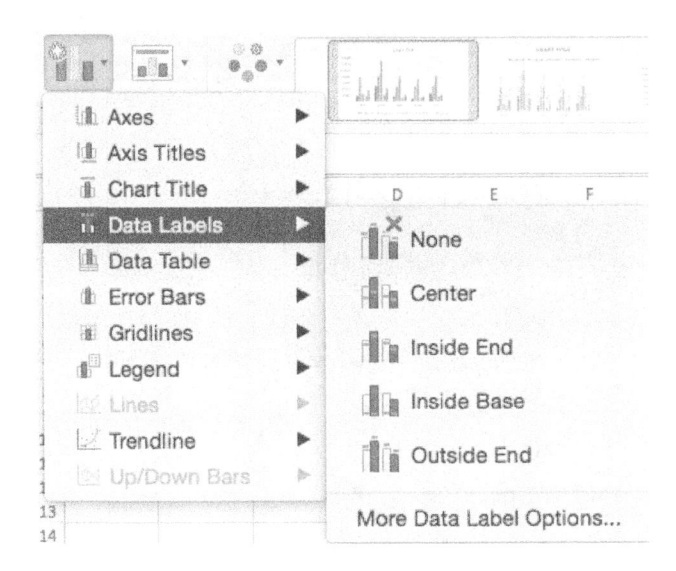

Each of the four choices will apply unique labels to each data point in your chart. Select your required option. Adding data labels to a clustered column chart, on the other hand, will appear cluttered. For instance, if you choose "Center" data labels, they will present like this:

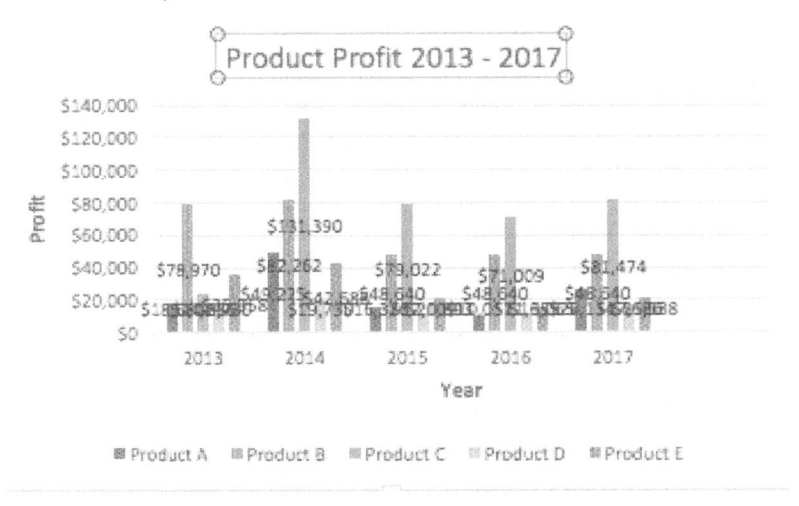

To Add a Data Table:

1. Select "Data Table" from the "Add Chart Element" menu. By selecting "More Data Table Options," you can access three pre-formatted options with an extended menu.

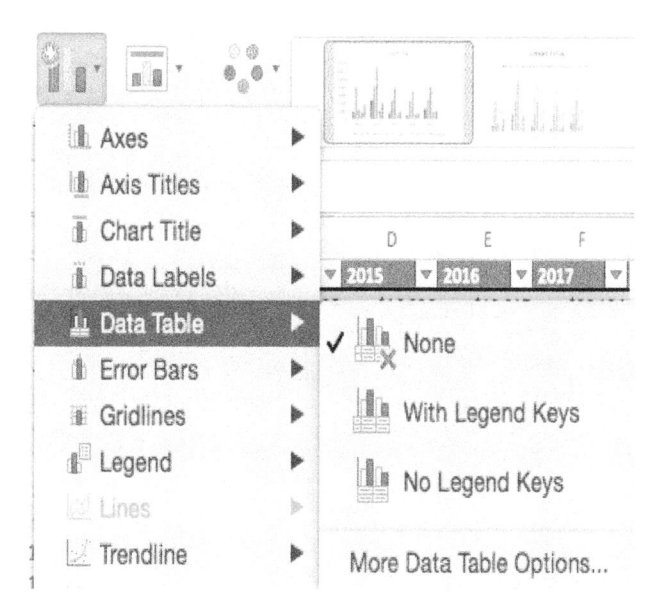

"Legend keys" show the data set by displaying the data table below the chart. The color-coded legend will also be added.

"None" is the default setting, where the data table is not recreated within the chart.

"No legend keys" also show the data table below the chart, but without the legend.

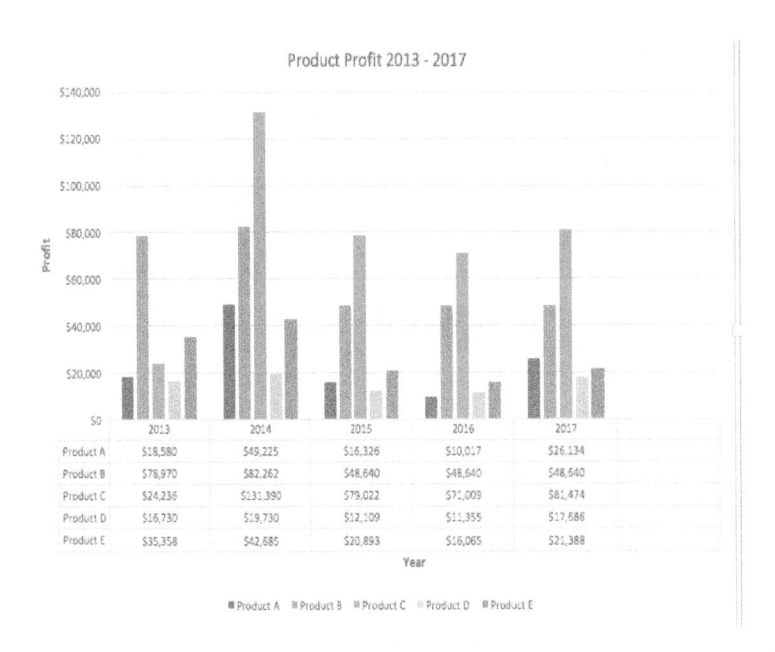

Note: If you want to add a data table, you'll probably need to expand your chart to make space for it. To resize your chart, simply click the corner and drag it to the required size.

To Add Error Bars:

1. Select "Error Bars" from the "Add Chart Element" menu. There are four options in addition to "More Error Bars Options": "Standard Error," "None" (default), "Standard Deviation," and 5% "Percentage." Using specific standard equations for segregating error, adding error bars provides a visual representation of the possible error in the displayed data.

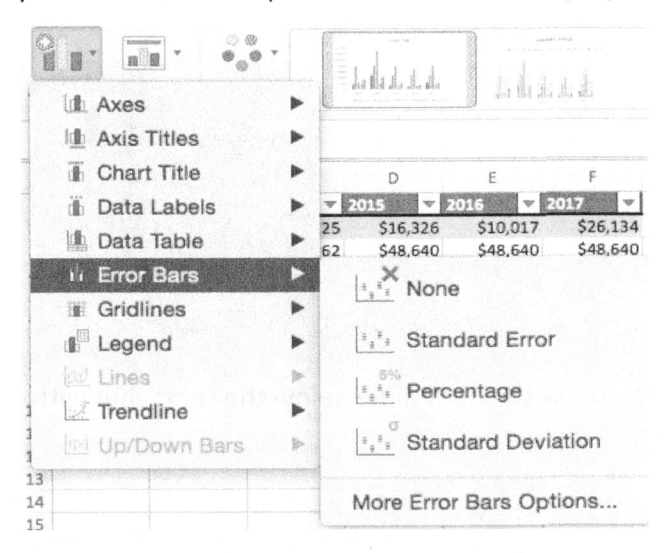

For instance, when we select "Standard Error" from the options, we obtain a chart similar to the one shown below:

Product Profit 2013 - 2017 chart

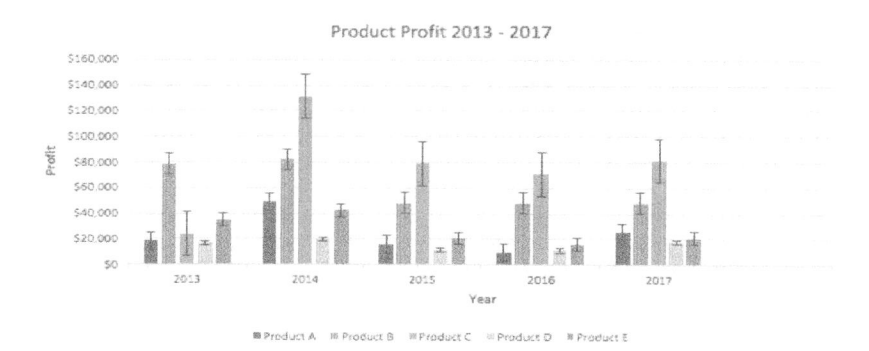

To Add Gridlines:

1. Select "Gridlines" from the "Add Chart Element" menu. There are four options in addition to "More Grid Line Options."
2. These options are "Primary Major Vertical," "Primary Major Horizontal," "Primary Minor Vertical," and "Primary Minor Horizontal." For a column chart, Excel will automatically add up "Primary Major Horizontal" gridlines.

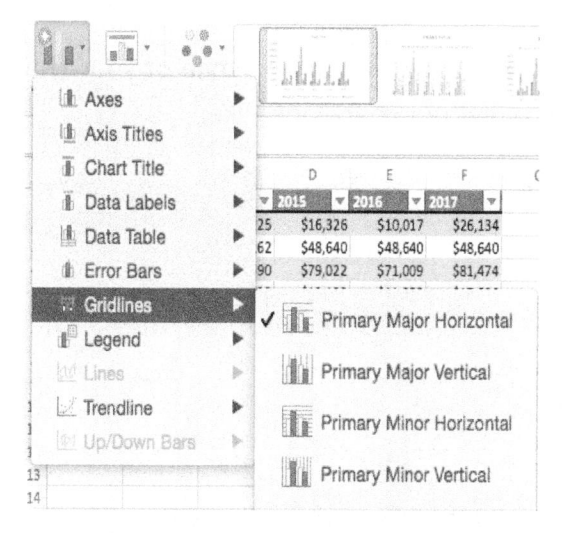

3. By clicking the options, you can choose different gridlines. For instance, when we select all four gridline options, our chart looks like this:

79 | EXCELL ACCELERATOR

To Add a Legend:

1. Select "Legend" from the "Add Chart Element" drop-down menu. There are five legend placement options in addition to "More Legend Options": "Right," "None," "Top," "Bottom," and "Left."

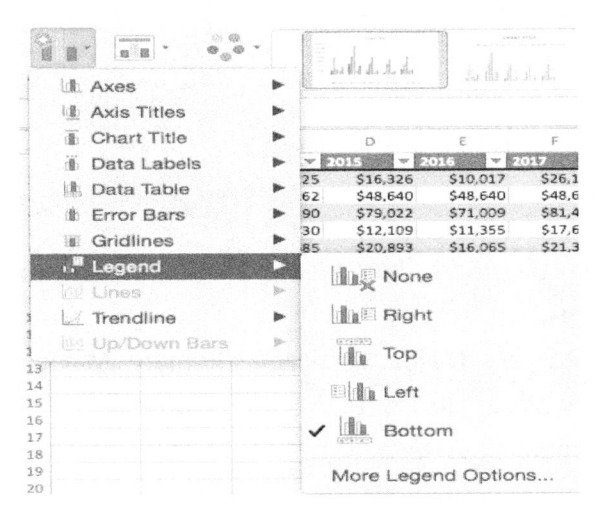

2. Legend placement will rely on the format and style of your chart. When we select the "Right" legend placement, this is what our chart looks like:

To Add Lines:

For clustered column charts, lines aren't available. But, in other chart forms where you are comparing two variables, you can add lines (e.g., reference, target, average, etc.) to the chart by implementing the required option.

To Add a Trendline:

1. Select "Trendline" from the "Add Chart Element" drop-down menu. There are five options in addition to "More Trendline Options": "Exponential," "None" (default), "Linear," "Moving

Average," and "Linear Forecast." For your data set, select the required option. We'll use the "Linear" option in this example:

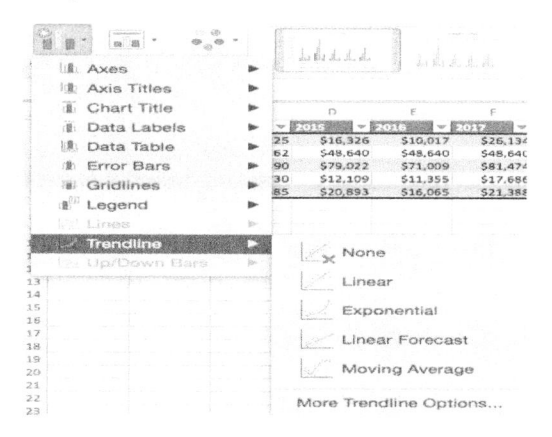

2. Excel will make a trendline for each product because we're comparing five different products over time. Click "Product A" and then click the blue "OK" button to create a linear trendline for it.

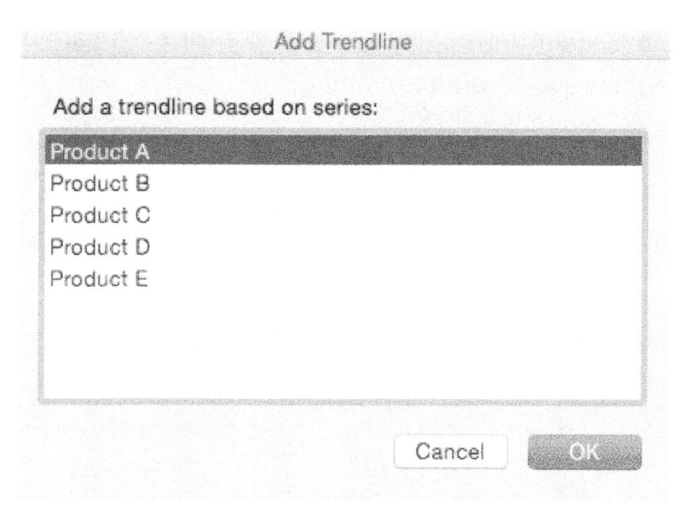

A dotted trendline will now appear on the chart to display Product A's linear progression. "Linear" (Product A) has also been added to the legend in Excel.

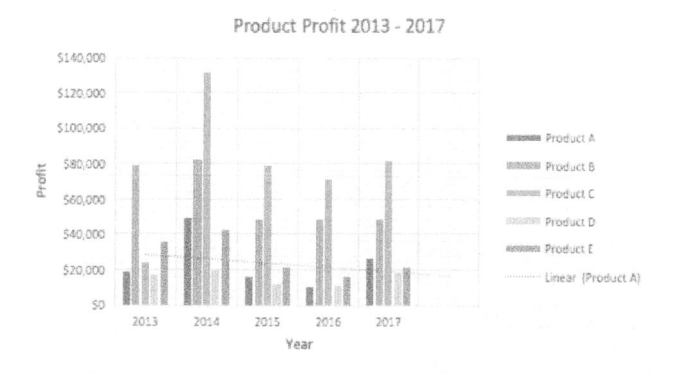

3. Double-click the trendline to show the trendline model on your chart.

81 | EXCELL ACCELERATOR

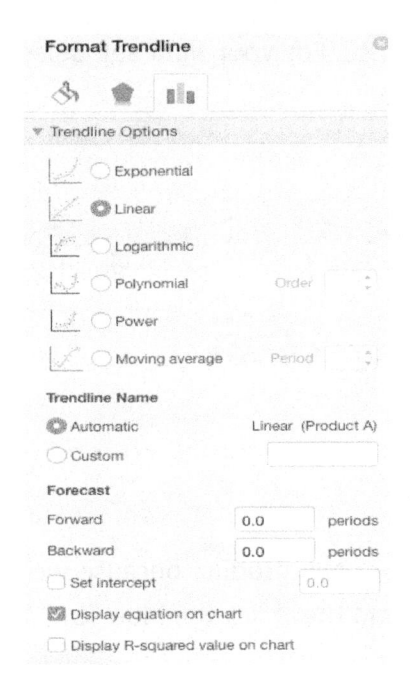

Note: You can make as many separate trendlines as you like for each variable in your chart. Here's an example of a chart with trendlines for Products A and C.

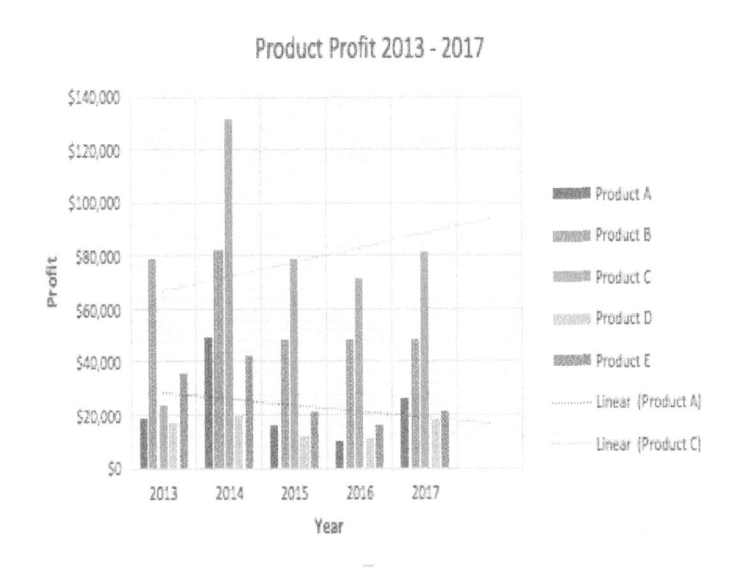

To Add Up/Down Bars:

In a column chart, "Up/Down Bars" are not available. But they can be used in a line chart to display increases and decreases between data points.

Step 4: Adjust Quick Layout

"Quick Layout" is the second drop-down menu on the toolbar. It helps you easily change the layout of your chart's components (legend, clusters, titles, etc.).

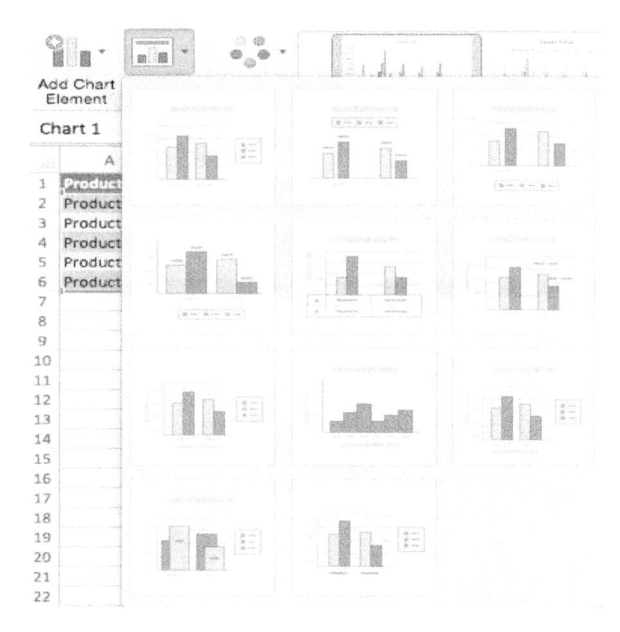

There are 11 quick layout options to choose from. Hover your cursor over the different possibilities for an explanation, then choose the one you want to use.

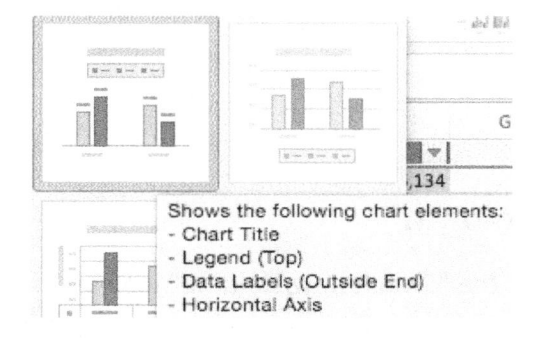

Step 5: Change Colors

"Change Colors" is the next drop-down menu in the toolbar. Click the icon, then select the color palette that best suits your needs (these needs have to match your brand's style and color and also be aesthetic).

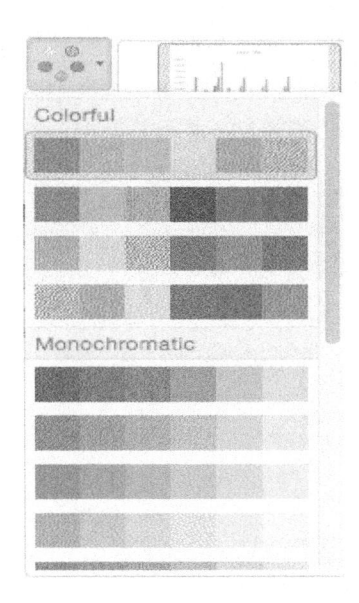

Step 6: Change Style

There are 14 chart styles available for cluster column charts. The chart will be displayed in "Style 1" by default, but you can modify it to any other style. To see other options, use the arrow on the right of the image bar.

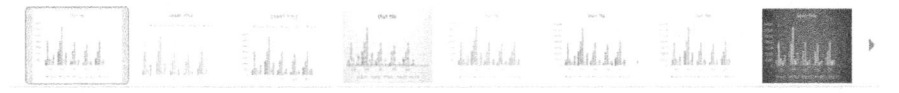

Step 7: Switch Row/Column

1. To switch the axes, select the "Switch Row/Column" icon on the toolbar. Note that flipping axes for every chart, particularly if there are more than two variables, is not always intuitive.

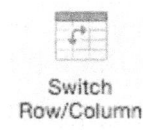

2. The product and year are swapped in this example by switching the row and column (profit remains on the y-axis). Click on the legend and alter the titles from "Series" to "Years" to prevent any confusion.

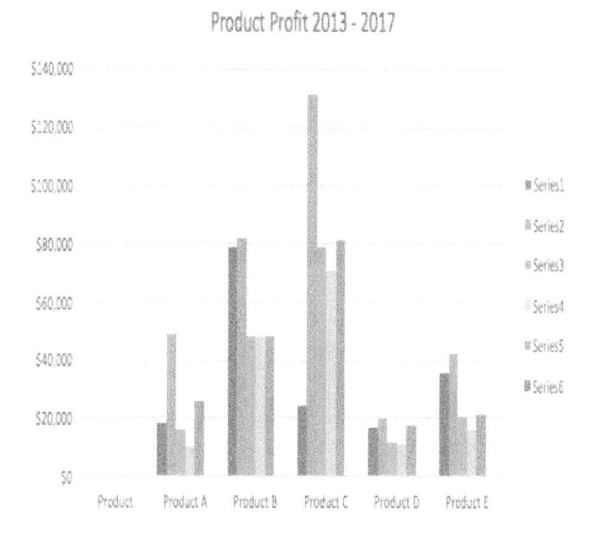

Step 8: Select Data

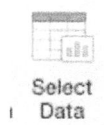

1. To adjust the range of your data, click the "Select Data" icon on the toolbar.
2. Then a window will open. Click the "OK" button after you've typed in the cell range you want. This new data range will be reflected in the chart automatically.

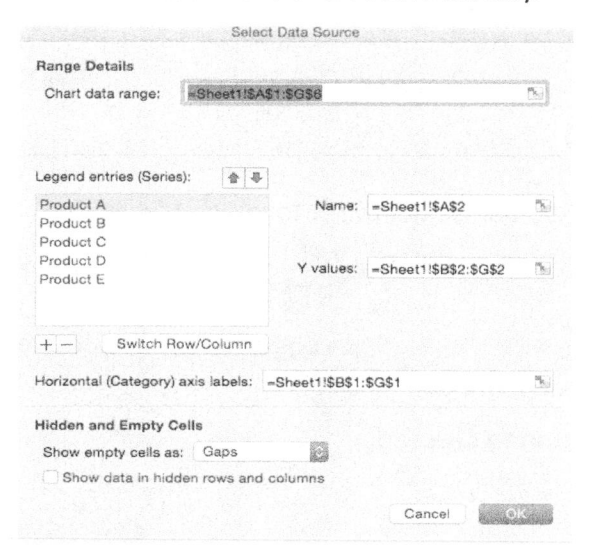

Step 9: Change Chart Type

1. From the dropdown menu, click the "Change Chart Type" icon.

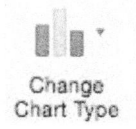

85 | EXCELL ACCELERATOR

2. You can change the chart type to any of Excel's nine chart categories from here. Make sure that your data is suitable for the chart type you've chosen.

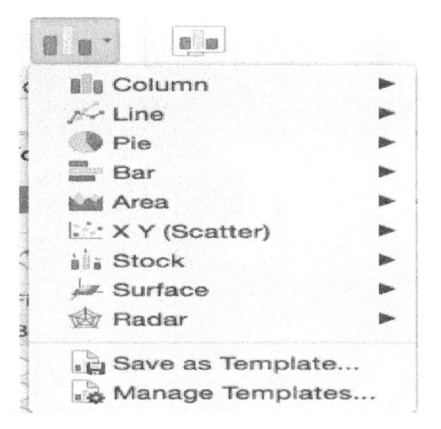

3. By selecting "Save as Template," you can also save your chart as a template.
4. To make it easier to arrange your templates, Excel will create a folder for them. To save your work, click the blue "Save" button.

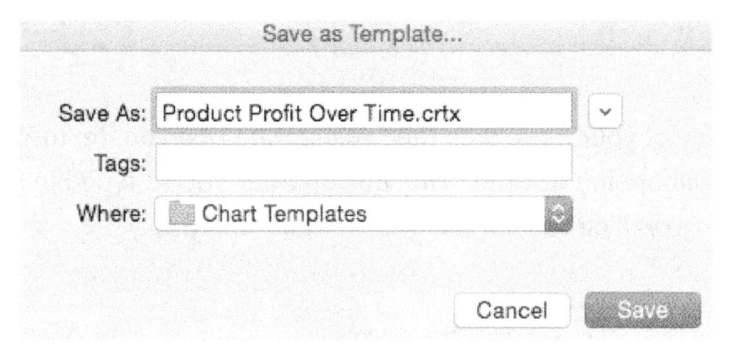

Step 10: Move Chart

1. On the far right of the toolbar, select the "Move Chart" icon.

2. Click the blue "OK" button to proceed.

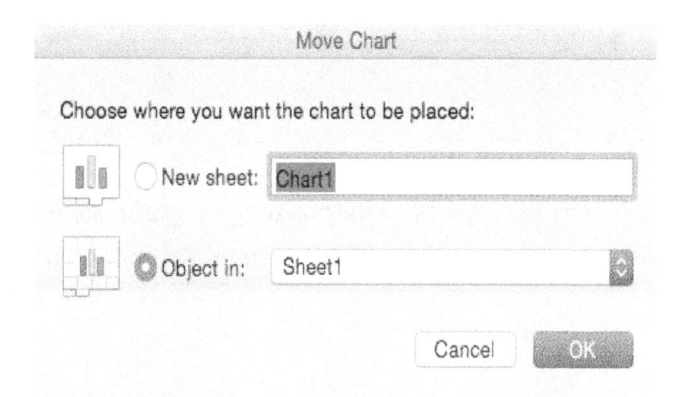

Step 11: Change Formatting

You can change the size, color, fill, shape, and alignment of all elements and text in the chart. You can also insert shapes using the "Format" tab.

1. To make a chart that reflects your organization's brand (images, colors, etc.), go to the "Format" tab and use the shortcuts available.

2. Select the chart element you want to edit from the drop-down menu on the top left side of the toolbar.

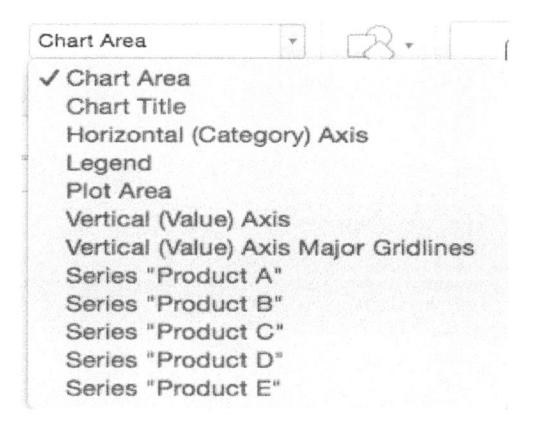

Step 12: Delete a Chart

1. Simply click a chart and press the "Delete" key on your keyboard to delete it.

How to Make a Graph in Excel

Despite the fact that charts and graphs are two different things, Excel groups graph into the chart categories.

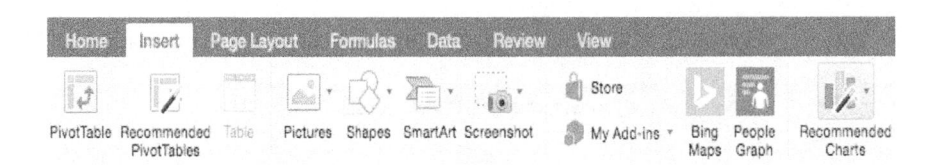

You now have a graph on your screen. You can customize your graph by following the steps described in the previous section. All features for creating a chart remain the same when making a graph.

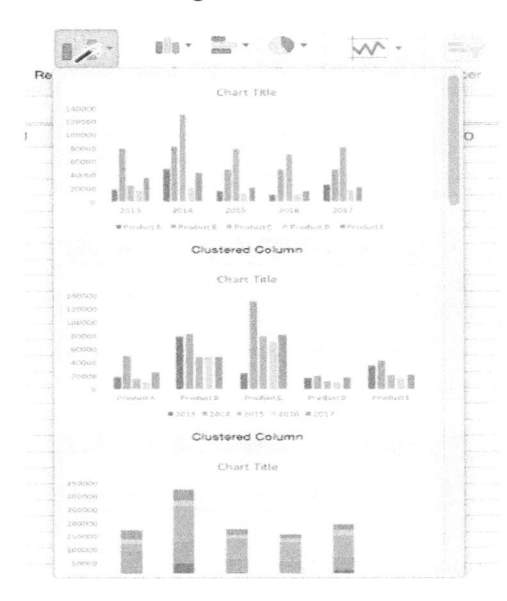

CHAPTER 4:
Data Importation (CSV, Text File)

Data Importation from Different Sources in Workbook

1. Go to "Data" and click "Get Data" from a "Data" tab.
2. Then choose "Workbook" from the "File" menu.

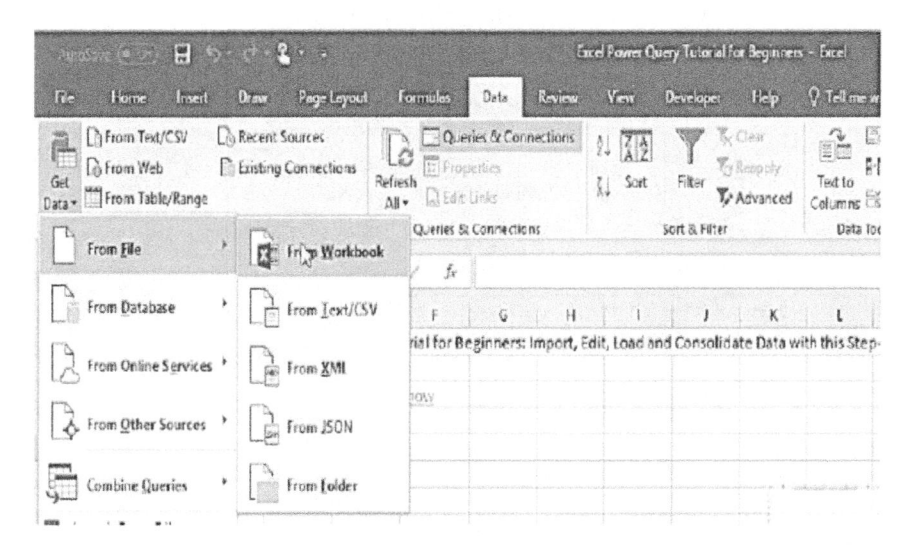

3. Find the "Workbook" in the "Import Data" dialog box and double-click it.

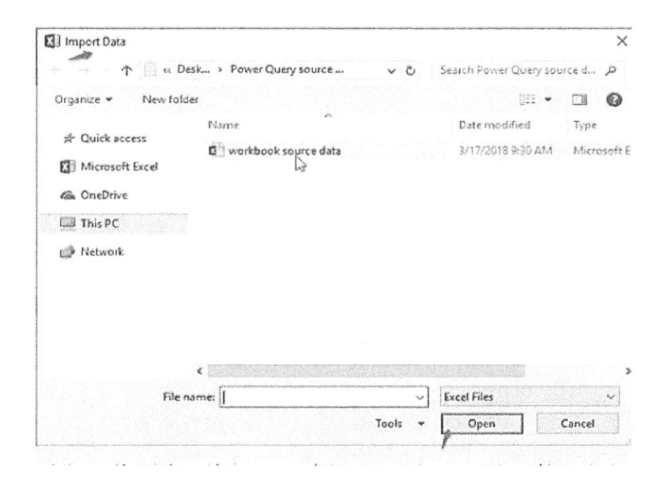

Data Import out of a CSV File:

1. Go over to "Data" and click "Get Data" from a "Data" tab.
2. Then pick "Text/CVS" from the "File" menu.

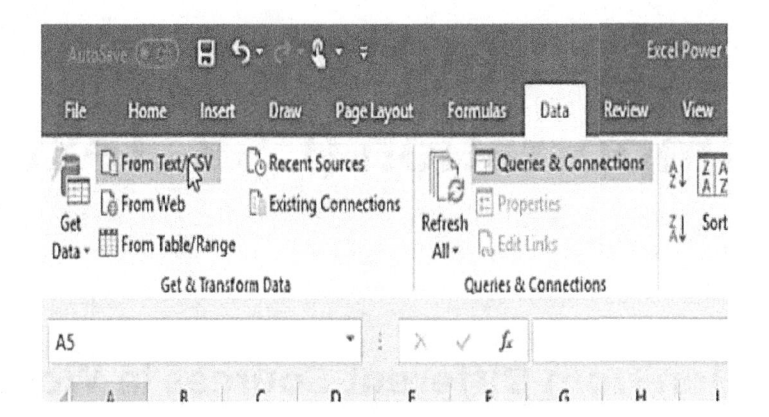

Data Import from Text File:

1. Go over to "Data" and click "Get Data" from the "Data" tab.
2. Then pick "Text/CVS" from the "File" menu.

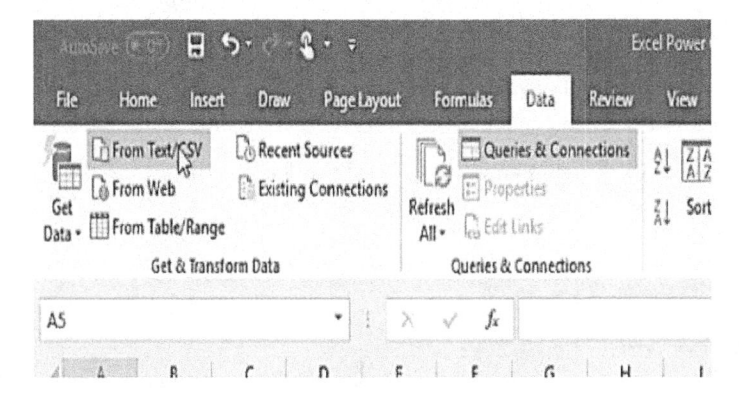

CHAPTER 5:
Pivot Table and Vlookup

Creating Excel Tables

The "Table" command can be used in Excel to translate data collection into a formatted Excel table. These tables have several features that will help you manage and display your results, such as filtering and sorting.

	A	B	C	D	E	F	G	H
1	Product Sales							
3	Dat	Region	Produ	Qty	Cost	Amt	Tax	Total
4	1-Apr	East	Paper	73	12.95	945.35	66.17	1,011.52
5	2-Apr	West	Pens	40	2.19	87.60	6.13	93.73
6	1-Apr	West	Paper	33	12.95	427.35	29.91	457.26
7	3-Apr	East	Paper	21	12.95	271.95	19.04	290.99
8	2-Apr	East	Pens	14	2.19	30.66	2.15	32.81
9	3-Apr	West	Paper	10	12.95	129.50	9.07	138.57

Excel Table Benefits and Drawbacks

It is easy to format a list as a called Excel table, and it has a lot of advantages and just a few disadvantages.

Benefits

- When you add or delete rows of data, the table's range immediately expands and contracts.
- Built-in styles make it simple to format or alter the appearance of the table.
- Formulas and formatting are automatically filled down.
- Structured references to table cells are used in formulas to display the column's name. This makes them simple to understand.
- Hide or show the table's built-in "Totals" row, which displays a "Count," "Average," "Sum," or other summary amount using formulas.
- An Excel table is a great place to start when creating a "Pivot Table." If data is inserted or removed, you will not have to adjust the range.

Drawbacks

There are a few disadvantages of using named Excel tables, so there might be times that you would rather not use them. Following are some drawbacks of using Excel tables:

- Since structured references to table cells do not have an "absolute" setting, copying them around a column is a little more difficult.
- Tables on protected sheets do not expand automatically, even though the cells below the table are unlocked.
- If every sheet includes an Excel chart, you will not be able to copy, group, or move them.
- In a workbook of one or more Excel tables, "Custom Views" are not allowed.

Preparing Your Data

Follow these instructions for data organization before creating the formatted Excel "Table":

1. Rows and columns can be used to organize the records, with each row providing details for a certain record, such as an inventory transaction or sales order.
2. Each column in the first row of the list should have a brief, clear, and distinct heading.
3. Each list column should contain only one form of data, such as currency, dates, or text.
4. The data for one record, such as a sales order, should be listed in each row of the list. Include a unique identification for each line, such as an order number, if possible.
5. There should be no blank rows on the list and no columns that are completely empty.
6. With one empty column and one empty row, at least between the list and the other data on the worksheet, the list can be separated from the other data.

	A	B	C	D	E	F	G	H
1	Product Sales							
2								
3	Date	Region	Product	Qty	Cost	Amt	Tax	Total
4	1-Apr	East	Paper	73	12.95	945.35	66.17	1,011.52
5	1-Apr	West	Paper	33	12.95	427.35	29.91	457.26
6	2-Apr	East	Pens	14	2.19	30.66	2.15	32.81
7	2-Apr	West	Pens	40	2.19	87.60	6.13	93.73
8	3-Apr	East	Paper	21	12.95	271.95	19.04	290.99
9	3-Apr	West	Paper	10	12.95	129.50	9.07	138.57

Create an Excel Table

You are ready to create the formatted table after you have organized the data as mentioned above.

1. Select a cell from the data list you prepared.

2. Click the "Insert" tab from the "Ribbon."

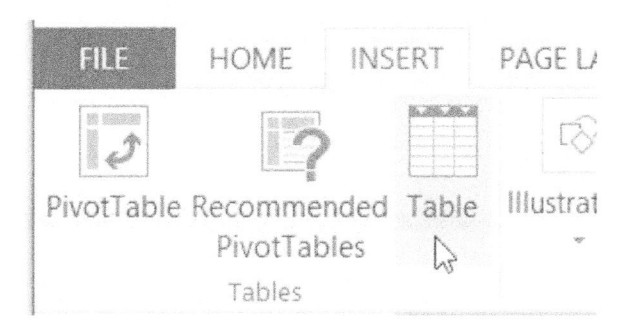

3. Select the "Table" command from the "Tables" group.
4. The range for your data should appear automatically in the "Create Table" dialogue box, and the table has a headers option that should be checked. You can change the range and check the box if necessary.
5. To accept these settings, click "OK."

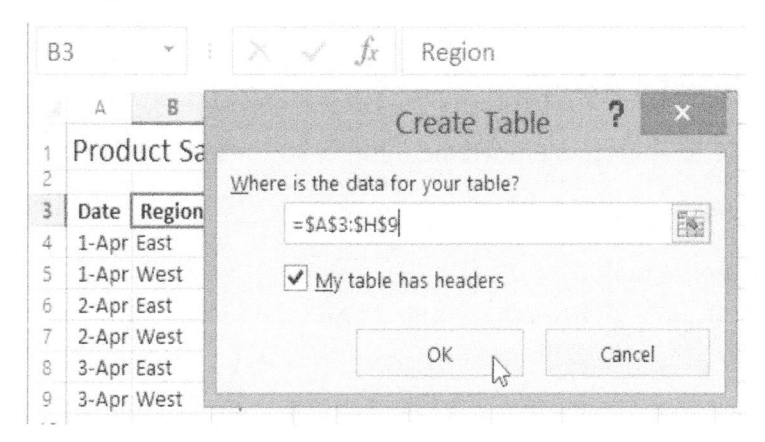

Sort and Filter the Data

Your list has now been transformed to an Excel table, which you may modify with a default "Table Style." You may sort or filter the data using the drop-down arrows in the heading cells.

Note: Excel "Table Slicers" can easily filter table data in Excel 2013 and later versions.

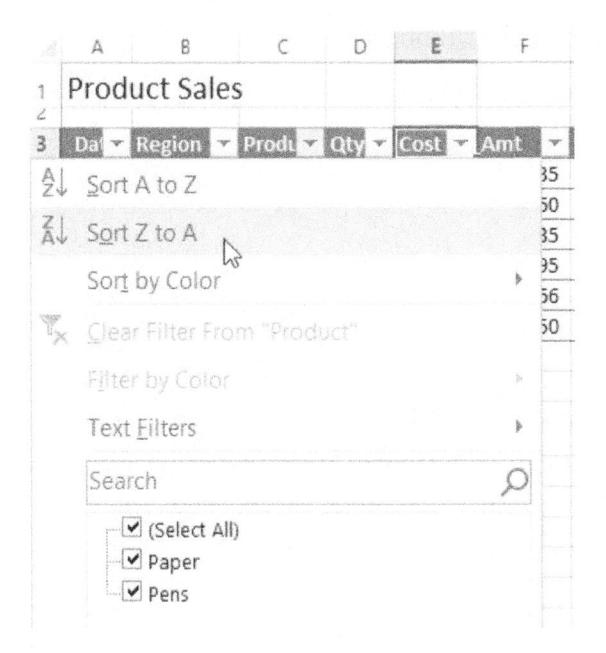

Rename an Excel Table

You can rename the table to something more meaningful so that you can deal with it more easily later.

To change the table name:

1. Select a cell in the table.
2. Select the "Design" tab from the "Table Tools" tab on the Ribbon.

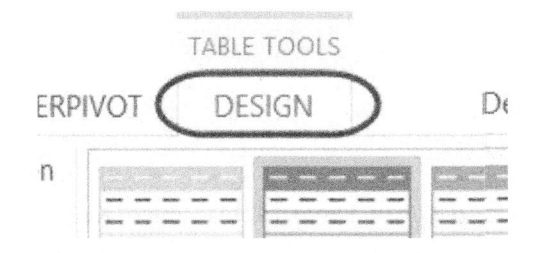

3. Click the existing name in the "Table Name" box on the far left of the Ribbon.

4. Then, using the "Enter" key, type a new name, such as "Orders."

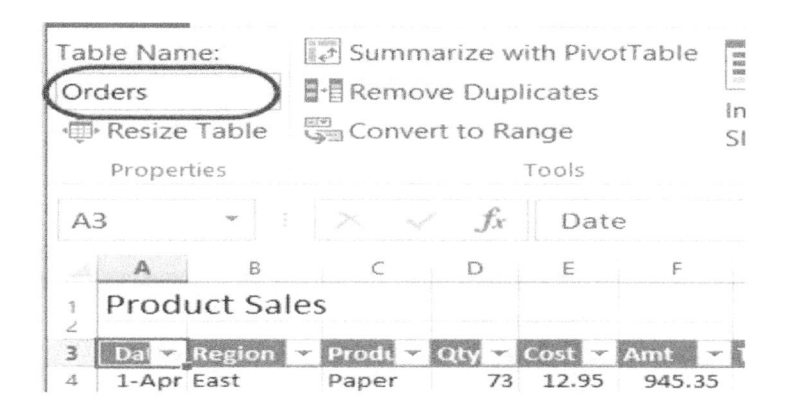

Create Excel Table with Specific Style

Instead of utilizing the default style, you can add a specific style from the "Table Style" options while creating a table. Then, when implementing the style, click the option to delete a current cell format from the data range.

Create an Excel Table in Excel with a Specific Style

If you choose to add a particular table style to an Excel table, follow these steps:

1. Select a cell from the data list you prepared.
2. Select the "Home" tab from the Ribbon.
3. Select "Format" as "Table" from the "Styles" group.
4. Select the style you want to use.

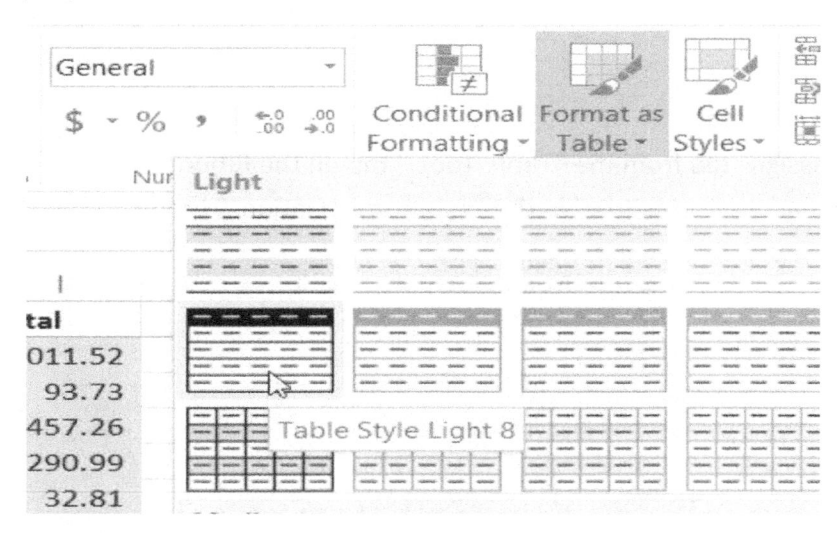

5. Or, right-click on a style and select "Apply and Clear Formatting" to apply the style and remove any current formatting.

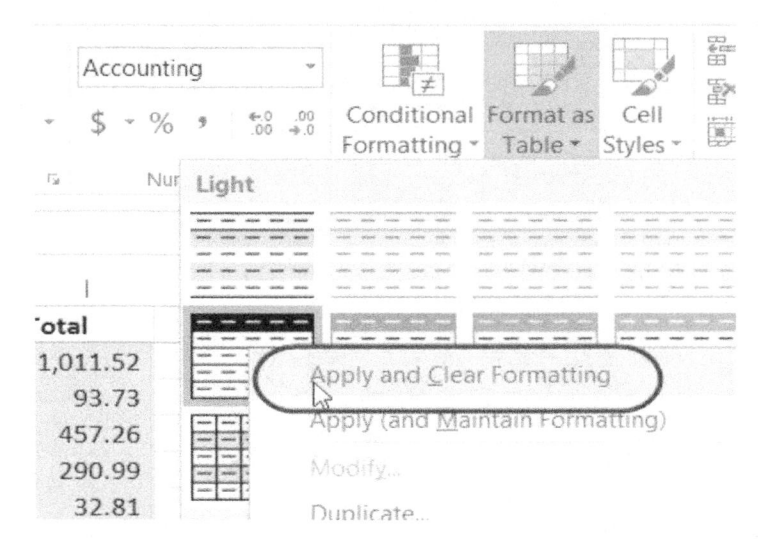

6. The range for your data should appear immediately in the "Create Table" dialogue box, and the table has headers choices that should be checked. You can change the range and check the box if desired.
7. To accept these settings, click "OK."

Note: The chosen table style is used to generate a formatted Excel table.

Show Totals in a Table

Using the built-in "Table" feature, you can easily display the total for a column or several columns after you have created an Excel table:

To Display a Total:

1. Select a cell in the table.
2. Select the "Design" tab from the "Table Tools" tab on the Ribbon.
3. Add a checkmark to "Total Row" in the "Table Style Options" group.

At the bottom of the table, a "Total" row will be added, and a total will be shown in one or more than one column of numbers.

Modify and Add Totals

Totals for other columns can be selected in addition to the ones that are generated automatically.

1. Select one of the columns and click on the Total cell.
2. Select the function you wish to use in the current column from the drop-down list.

The cell is given the "SUBTOTAL" formula, which displays the calculation in the table's column depending on the visible cells.

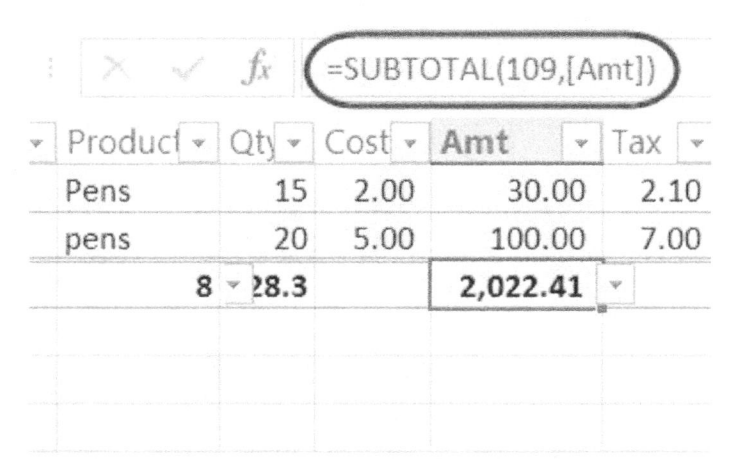

Refer to any Table Column in a Formula

A "Structured Reference" is provided when a formula refers to a named Excel table. The table's column name and the table name will be shown in the "Structured Reference."

Formula Outside the Table

A formula would be generated outside of the table in this example. The "COUNTBLANK" function will be used in the formula to count the blank cells in a table column. "Ordered" is the table name, and "Product" is the column name.

1. Type "=COUNTBLANK" in a blank cell to start the formula.

2. Then, for the column you want to check, click at the very top of the heading cell; the cursor would change to a down arrow.

3. Do not click on the column button where the column letter is.

4. Also, do not click in the middle of a heading cell.

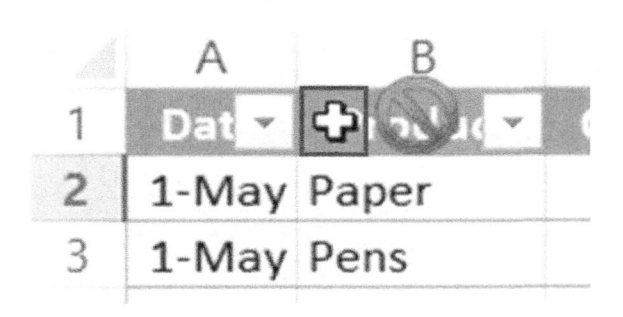

5. The table name and column name should be shown in the structured reference: "COUNTBLANK (Orders [Product])."

6. Type a closing bracket, then press the "Enter" key in order to complete the formula.

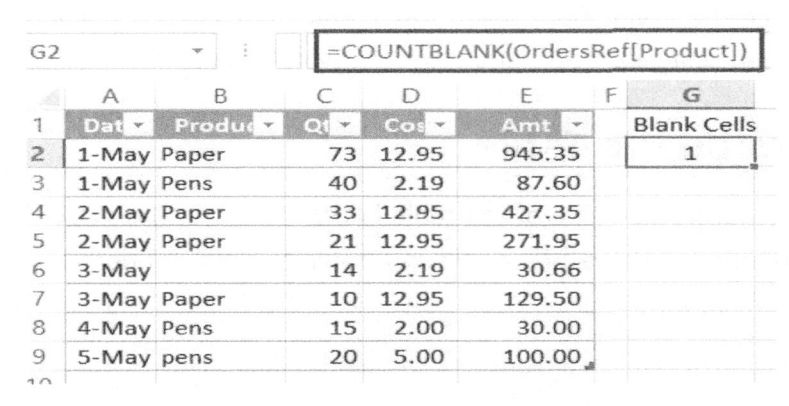

Add a Counter Field

Add a counter field to the Excel table if you want to use it as the source information for a pivot table. It may be used in summary calculations or calculated fields.

If instead of typing the value, you use a simple formula, this is quite simple to generate and manage in an Excel table.

1. In the first blank column of the orders table sheet, add the heading "Sales."
2. To complete the formula, press "Enter."

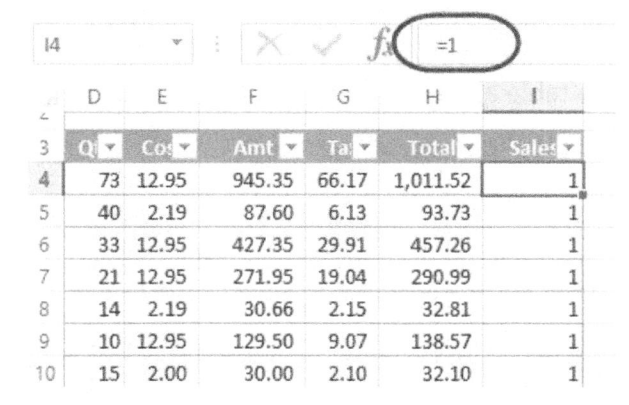

Q	Cost	Amt	Tax	Total	Sales
73	12.95	945.35	66.17	1,011.52	1
40	2.19	87.60	6.13	93.73	1
33	12.95	427.35	29.91	457.26	1
21	12.95	271.95	19.04	290.99	1
14	2.19	30.66	2.15	32.81	1
10	12.95	129.50	9.07	138.57	1
15	2.00	30.00	2.10	32.10	1

The formula would immediately fill down all the rows since the data is in a named Excel table. When you add new rows, they will also be automatically entered.

The 1s can provide a value-added together in a pivot table or used in a "Calculated Field" to provide accurate results.

Print Excel Table Only

When dealing with lists in Excel, make use of the built-in "Table" feature to make data manipulation simpler. Then, if you want to print the table and not the other worksheet items, you may use a built-in command called "Print List."

Since the command is not on the Ribbon, you may either add it or add it to the "Quick Access Toolbar."

Using Pivot Tables in Excel

"Conventional Excel" tables, which are sometimes too inflexible for anyone who may analyze large amounts of data, reach their limits quickly. Pivot tables with advanced features are the ideal option. Pivot tables in Excel show their maximum ability to interpret and prepare data. They may be used to compress data and refine the presentation as required on a case-by-case basis.

Pivot tables do simpler work that is normally complicated with traditional tables. Pivot tables enable users to adjust the way data is displayed without having to change the data themselves. The basis for this is often a separate, very simple-looking table that holds the whole data collection. Additional functions in "Pivot" enable the data to be sorted, filtered, and presented in various ways.

The idea that the data can only be displayed independently is an essential aspect of learning pivot Excel. Changes to the pivot table would not add additional data to the initial spreadsheet (for example, duplicate data) or erase old data (for example, if the data is filtered).

Creating a Pivot Table

As soon as you learn how pivot works, creating a pivot table in Excel is easy. A pivot table is often built on a set of data with several columns. The name of the respective division must appear in the first row of the column. This is where the pivot table gets its data from. It's also a good idea to use the "Format as Table" feature to format the table and give it a name. This makes the process simpler—mainly when dealing with several data sets.

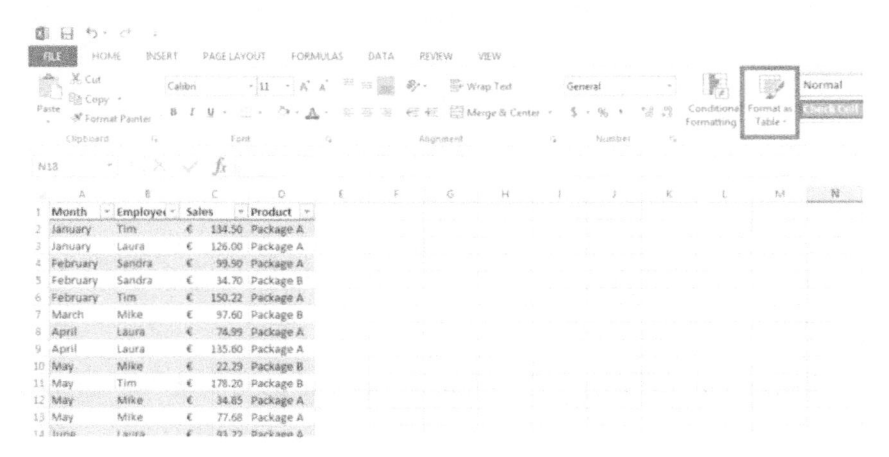

Excel's pivot table is built on a data set. To make things easy to work with, convert this into a table.

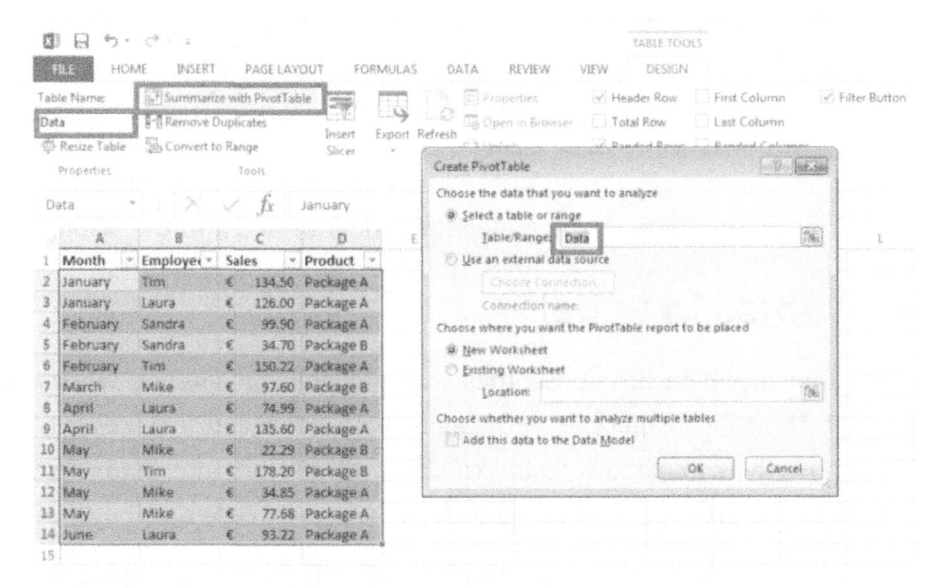

Go to "Pivot Tables Field Panel" and click the field name checkbox to add a field to the pivot table. If you choose to shift the field from one place to another, drag it with your mouse to the desired spot.

The Pivot Chart

The pivot chart is a visual representation of the pivot table's results. Follow the steps below to generate a pivot chart from a pivot table:

1. In the pivot table, choose a cell.
2. Choose "Pivot Chart" from the "Insert" menu.
3. Then select "OK."

Using Slicer on Pivot tables and Tables

To filter content on tables or Pivot tables, use the slicer feature. It appears to be a button on the Excel worksheet that allows you to sort results.

1. Choose any cell on the table or pivot table to use the slicer.
2. Choose "Slicer" from the "Insert" menu on the "Home" page.
3. Select the area you wish to view from the checks box in the "Insert Slicers" dialogue box.
4. Then press the "OK" button.

The VLOOKUP Function

The "VLOOKUP" feature in Excel allows you to look up a specific piece of data in a table or data collection and retrieve the associated data/information. In plain English, the "VLOOKUP" feature tells Excel to "look for this piece of information (e.g., bananas) in this data collection (a table) and tell me any corresponding information about it (e.g., banana price)."

The formula is:

=VLOOKUP (lookup value, table array, col index num, [range lookup])

To put it in another way, the formula says, "Find this piece of information in the following field and send me some matching details from another column." The following arguments are passed to the VLOOKUP function:

1. **Lookup value (Necessary Argument):** Lookup value defines the value in the first column of a table that we want to look up.
2. **Table Array (Necessary Argument):** The table array represents the data array to be scanned. The VLOOKUP feature looks in the array's left-most column.
3. **Col Index Num (Necessary Argument):** This is an integer that specifies the column number of the supplied table array from which a value should be returned.
4. **Range Lookup (Selectable Argument):** This specifies what this feature can return if it cannot locate an exact match for the lookup value. The value of the statement may be "TRUE" or "FALSE," which means:

TRUE: Estimated match, which means that the nearest match below the lookup value is used if an exact match cannot be sought.

FALSE: Exact match; if an exact match is not detected, an error would be returned.

How to Use VLOOKUP in Excel?

Sort the Information: The first step in utilizing the VLOOKUP feature is to ensure your data is well-organized and appropriate for it. Since VLOOKUP operates from left to right, you must ensure that the data you wish to look up is to the left of the data you want to extract.

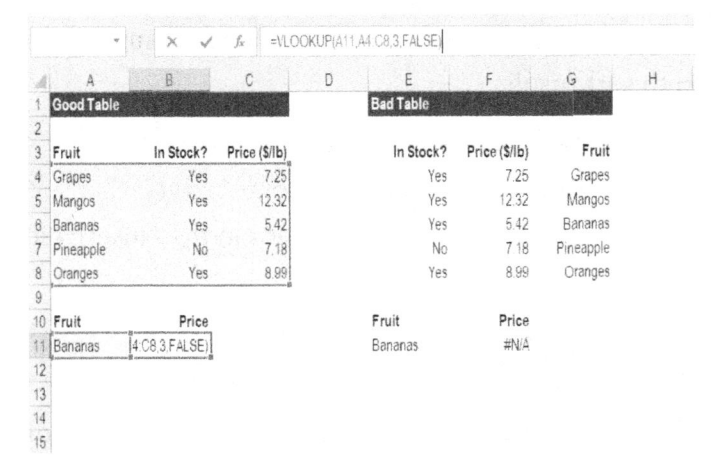

Since bananas are in the leftmost column in the above VLOOKUP illustration, the "Healthy Table" will quickly run the function to look up "Bananas" and return their price. There is an error message in the "Bad Table" case because the columns are not in the correct sequence. This is one of VLOOKUP's most significant flaws, and It's for this purpose that "INDEX MATCH" can be used instead of "VLOOKUP."

Tell the Function What to Look up: We say Excel what to see for in this process. First, type the formula "=VLOOKUP," and then select a cell comprising the data we want to look up. It's the cell that says "Bananas" in this situation.

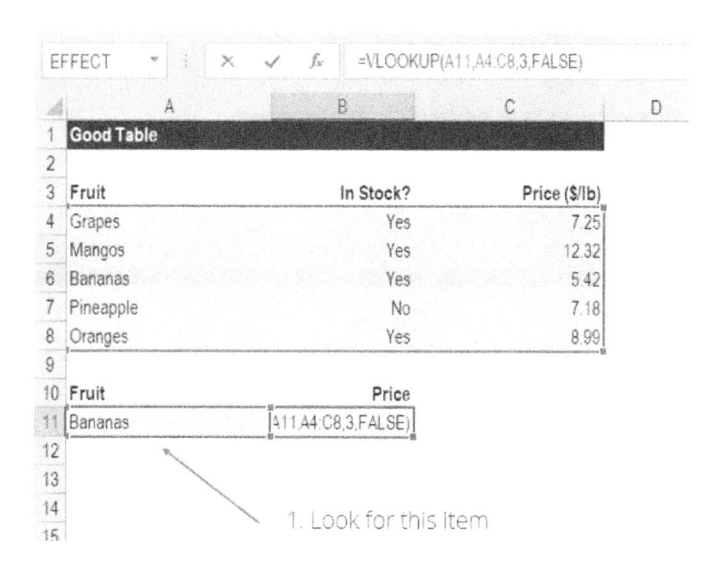

[Screenshot showing Excel VLOOKUP formula =VLOOKUP(A11,A4:C8,3,FALSE) with a "Good Table" of fruits, In Stock? status, and Price ($/lb). Arrow labeled "1. Look for this item" points to A11 "Bananas".]

Tell the Function Where to Look: In this stage, we select the table containing the data and instruct Excel to look for the details we choose in the previous phase in the leftmost column. In this example, we've highlighted the entire table from column A to column C. Excel would search in column A for the details we told it to look up.

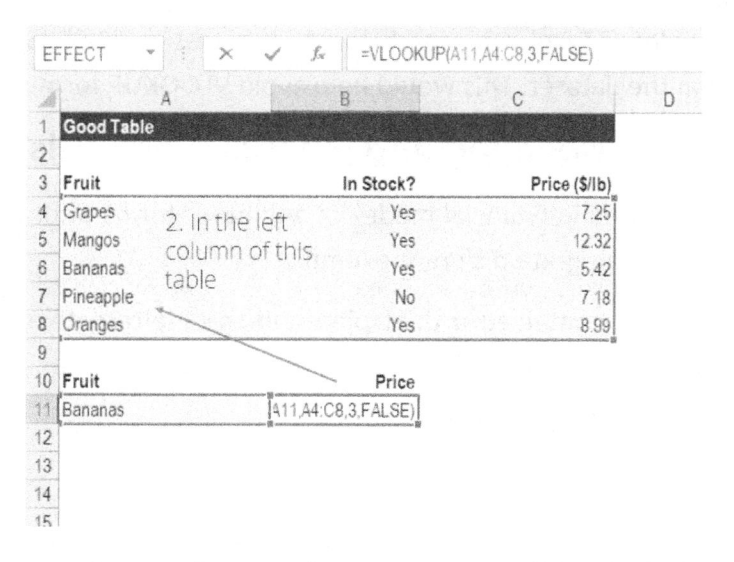

[Screenshot showing the same Excel sheet with the table A4:C8 highlighted. Arrow labeled "2. In the left column of this table" points to the table.]

Tell Excel Where Column to Output the Data from: We must tell Excel which column contains the data we want to provide as an output from the VLOOKUP. Excel would require a number that correlates to the table's column number. Since the output data is in the third column of the table in our case, we use the number "3" in the formula.

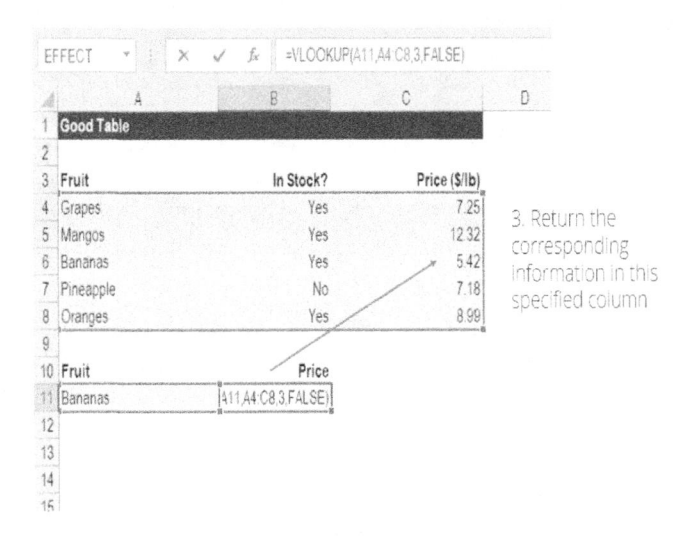

Approximate or Same Exact Match: By entering "False" or "True" in the formula, you can tell Excel if you're searching for an exact or estimated match. We want the same or exact match ("Bananas") in our VLOOKUP function formula example, so we type "False" in the formula. We might get a close match if we used "True" as a factor instead.

When looking up an actual statistic that isn't in the table, for example, the number "2.9585," an estimated match will be helpful. Excel can search for the nearest to "2.9585" in this situation, even though that number isn't in the dataset. This would help avoid VLOOKUP formula errors.

VLOOKUP in Financial Modeling and Financial Analysis

VLOOKUP formulas are often used in financial modeling and other forms of financial analysis to render simulations more complex and integrate different examples.

Consider a financial model that contained a debt plan and three alternative interest rate scenarios: 3.0%, 4.0%, and 5.0%. A VLOOKUP could look for a low, medium, or high scenario and then output the associated interest rate into the financial model.

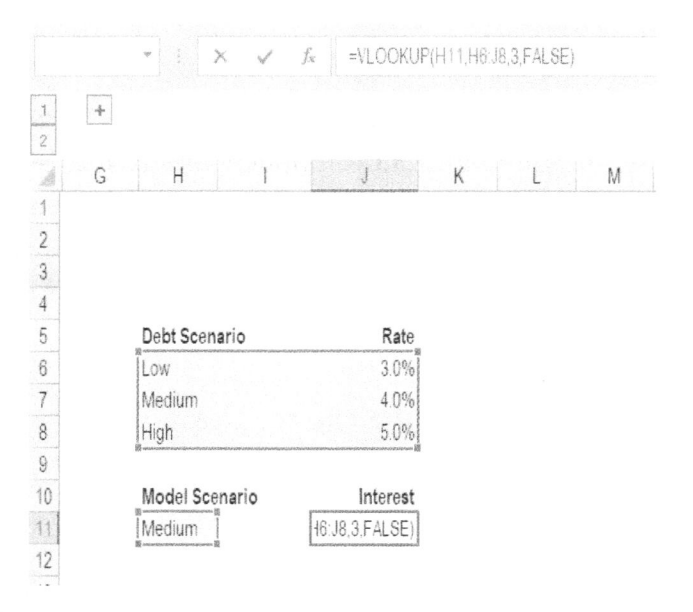

Tips for the VLOOKUP Function

The following is a set of essential items to note regarding the "Excel VLOOKUP Function":

- The VLOOKUP feature would allow a non-exact match if the lookup range is omitted, but it would use an exact match if one existed.
- The function's most significant flaw is that it still seems to be right. It can pull data from the columns to the right of the table's first node.
- VLOOKUP can only fit the first value if the lookup column includes redundant values.
- The role is unaffected by the situation.
- Assume that a VLOOKUP formula already exists in a worksheet. In that case, if we add a column to the table, formulas will split. Since hard-coded column index values do not adjust immediately as columns are added or removed, this is the case.
- Assume the table we're dealing with has numbers inserted as text in the function. It doesn't matter whether we're only extracting numbers as text from a table panel. However, we'll get a "#N/A!" if the table's first column includes numbers entered as text. If the lookup value is not indeed in text type, an error will occur.
- If the VLOOKUP function fails to locate a fit for the supplied lookup value, an error is returned ("#NONE").
- The error "#REF Error" occurs whenever one or more of the following conditions are met: The number of columns in the supplied table array is greater than the "col index num" argument, or the formula tried to appeal to cells that did not function.
- The error "#WORTH. Error" occurs whenever one or more of the following conditions are met: "The col_index num" statement is less than one or isn't a numeric value, or the "range_lookup" statement isn't understood as a "TRUE" or "FALSE" logical value.

"VLOOKUP" and "#N/A" Errors

If you use VLOOKUP, you'll almost certainly get a "#N/A" warning. The error code "#N/A" simply indicates "not identified." All the three VLOOKUP formulas return into "#N/A" if the lookup cost or value for "Toy Story 2" did not appear in the lookup table on the screen given below:

One method to "trap" the "N/A" error is to use the "IFNA" function like below:

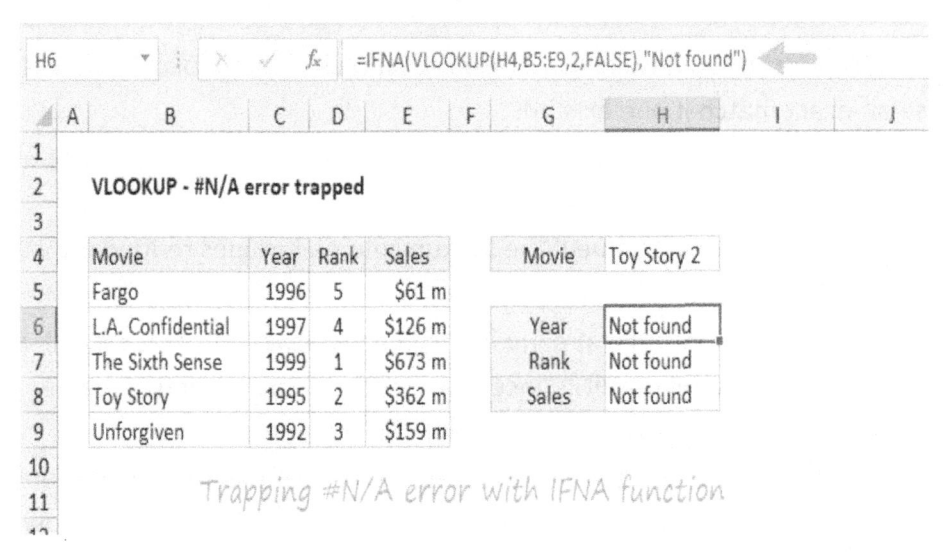

H6 shows the formula which is "= IFNA" and "VLOOKUP (H4, B5; E9, 2, FALSE)," "Not found"

This error will tell you that

- The lookup formula is misspelled or includes extra space in the table.
- The match mode is the same rather than should be approximate.
- The table set is not inserted correctly.
- The "Copy" of VLOOKUP and the table relation are not locked.

BONUS:
50 complex formulas to streamline your daily work

No	Formula	Description	Example
1	=VLOOKUP(A2,Sheet2!A2:B100,2,FALSE)	Look up a value in another table	=VLOOKUP("Product1",Sheet2!A2:B100,2,FALSE)
2	=SUMIFS(B2:B100,A2:A100,"Category1")	Sum values based on multiple conditions	=SUMIFS(B2:B100,A2:A100,"Category1")
3	=INDEX(Sheet2!B2:B100,MATCH(A2,Sheet2!A2:A100,0))	Index and match for exact value lookup	=INDEX(Sheet2!B2:B100,MATCH("ValueX",Sheet2!A2:A100,0))
4	=CONCATENATE(A2," - ",B2)	Combine text from multiple cells	=CONCATENATE("Name: ",A2," - Score: ",B2)
5	=IF(ISBLANK(A2),"No Data",A2)	Replace blank cells with custom text	=IF(ISBLANK(A2),"No Data","Has Data")
6	=AVERAGEIFS(C2:C100,B2:B100,"Category1")	Calculate average based on multiple conditions	=AVERAGEIFS(C2:C100,B2:B100,"Category1")
7	=TEXT(DATE(2023,3,15),"dd-mmm-yyyy")	Format date as "15-Mar-2023"	=TEXT(DATE(2023,3,15),"dd-mmm-yyyy")
8	=COUNTIF(B2:B100,"Complete")	Count cells with specific text	=COUNTIF(B2:B100,"Completed")
9	=MAX(D2:D100)-MIN(D2:D100)	Calculate the range between maximum and minimum	=MAX(D2:D100)-MIN(D2:D100)

	Formula	Description	Example
10	=IF(AND(A2="Yes",B2>100), "Qualified", "Not Qualified")	Combine logical conditions	=IF(AND(A2="Yes",B2>100),"Qualified","Not Qualified")
11	=SUMPRODUCT((A2:A100="Category1")*(C2:C100))	Sum based on criteria using SUMPRODUCT	=SUMPRODUCT((A2:A100="Category1")*(C2:C100))
12	=INDEX(Sheet2!C2:C100,MATCH(MAX(Sheet2!B2:B100),Sheet2!B2:B100,0))	Index and match for maximum value	=INDEX(Sheet2!C2:C100,MATCH(MAX(Sheet2!B2:B100),Sheet2!B2:B100,0))
13	=ROUNDUP(B2,0)	Round up to nearest whole number	=ROUNDUP(123.456,0)
14	=IFERROR(VLOOKUP(A2,Sheet2!A2:B100,2,FALSE),"N/A")	Handle errors with custom text	=IFERROR(VLOOKUP("ValueX",Sheet2!A2:B100,2,FALSE),"Data not found")
15	=COUNTIFS(A2:A100,"Category1",B2:B100,"Complete")	Count cells based on multiple criteria	=COUNTIFS(A2:A100,"Category1",B2:B100,"Complete")
16	=SUMPRODUCT((MONTH(A2:A100)=3)*(C2:C100))	Sum values based on a specific month	=SUMPRODUCT((MONTH(A2:A100)=3)*(C2:C100))
17	=NETWORKDAYS(DATE(2023,3,1),DATE(2023,3,31),Sheet2!A2:A10)	Calculate working days between two dates	=NETWORKDAYS(DATE(2023,3,1),DATE(2023,3,31),Sheet2!A2:A10)
18	=SUBTOTAL(9,C2:C100)	Calculate sum ignoring hidden rows	=SUBTOTAL(9,C2:C100)
19	=RANK(B2,$B$2:$B$100)	Calculate the rank of a value in a range	=RANK(B2,$B$2:$B$100)
20	=TRANSPOSE(A2:D2)	Transpose rows into columns	=TRANSPOSE(A2:D2)
21	=AVERAGEIFS(C2:C100,A2:A100,"Category1")	Calculate average based on multiple conditions	=AVERAGEIFS(C2:C100,A2:A100,"Category1")
22	=IF(OR(B2="High",B2="Medium"), "Priority", "Low")	Combine logical conditions	=IF(OR(B2="High",B2="Medium"),"Priority","Low")

#	Formula	Description	Example
23	=SUMPRODUCT((A2:A100="Category1")(B2:B100="Complete")(C2:C100))	Sum based on multiple criteria	=SUMPRODUCT((A2:A100="Category1")(B2:B100="Complete")(C2:C100))
24	=INDEX(Sheet2!D2:D100,MATCH(MAX(Sheet2!C2:C100),Sheet2!C2:C100,0))	Index and match for maximum value	=INDEX(Sheet2!D2:D100,MATCH(MAX(Sheet2!C2:C100),Sheet2!C2:C100,0))
25	=IF(LEN(A2)>10, "Long Text", "Short Text")	Determine if text is long or short	=IF(LEN(A2)>10, "Long Text", "Short Text")
26	=IFERROR(AVERAGE(C2:C100),"No Data")	Handle errors in calculating average	=IFERROR(AVERAGE(C2:C100),"No Data")
27	=COUNTIFS(A2:A100,"Category1",C2:C100,">100")	Count cells based on multiple criteria	=COUNTIFS(A2:A100,"Category1",C2:C100,">100")
28	=TEXTJOIN(", ",TRUE,A2:A10)	Combine text from a range with delimiter	=TEXTJOIN(", ",TRUE,A2:A10)
29	=IF(OR(A2="Yes",B2="Yes"),"Both Yes","Not Both Yes")	Combine logical conditions	=IF(OR(A2="Yes",B2="Yes"),"Both Yes","Not Both Yes")
30	=SUMPRODUCT(--(TEXT(A2:A100,"mmm")="Mar")*(C2:C100))	Sum values based on specific month	=SUMPRODUCT(--(TEXT(A2:A100,"mmm")="Mar")*(C2:C100))
31	=IF(COUNTIF(B2:B100,B2)>1, "Duplicate", "Unique")	Identify duplicate values in a range	=IF(COUNTIF(B2:B100,B2)>1, "Duplicate", "Unique")
32	=INDEX(Sheet2!A2:A100,MODE(MATCH(Sheet2!A2:A100,Sheet2!A2:A100,0)))	Identify most frequent value	=INDEX(Sheet2!A2:A100,MODE(MATCH(Sheet2!A2:A100,Sheet2!A2:A100,0)))
33	=TEXT(A2,"dd-mmm-yyyy")	Format date as "15-Mar-2023"	=TEXT(A2,"dd-mmm-yyyy")
34	=IF(COUNTIF(A2:A100,A2)>1,"Duplicate","Unique")	Check for duplicate values	=IF(COUNTIF(A2:A100,A2)>1,"Duplicate","Unique")
35	=ROUND(A2,2)	Round number to 2 decimal places	=ROUND(123.456,2)

#	Formula	Description	Example
36	=IF(A2>100,"Above 100","Below 100")	Check if number is above or below 100	=IF(A2>100,"Above 100","Below 100")
37	=HYPERLINK("http://www.example.com/", "Click here")	Create a clickable hyperlink	=HYPERLINK("http://www.example.com/", "Click here")
38	=IF(LEN(A2)>50,LEFT(A2,50)&"...","A2")	Limit text length and add ellipsis	=IF(LEN(A2)>50,LEFT(A2,50)&"...","A2")
39	=SUMPRODUCT(--(ISNUMBER(FIND("Keyword",A2:A100))),C2:C100)	Sum values based on keyword match	=SUMPRODUCT(--(ISNUMBER(FIND("Keyword",A2:A100))),C2:C100)
40	=AGGREGATE(9,0,Sheet2!C2:C100/(Sheet2!A2:A100="Category1"))		=AGGREGATE(9,0,Sheet2!C2:C100/(Sheet2!A2:A100="Category1"))
41	=COUNTIFS(A2:A100,">="&DATE(2023,1,1),A2:A100,"<"&DATE(2023,2,1))	Calculate sum ignoring hidden rows with conditions	=COUNTIFS(A2:A100,">="&DATE(2023,1,1),A2:A100,"<"&DATE(2023,2,1))
42	=IF(A2="High",B21.1,IF(A2="Medium",B21.05,B2*1.02))	Count dates within a specific month	=IF(A2="High",B21.1,IF(A2="Medium",B21.05,B2*1.02))
43	=TRANSPOSE(SPLIT(A2," "))	Apply tiered percentage increase	=TRANSPOSE(SPLIT("John Doe"," "))
44	=SUBSTITUTE(A2,"old","new")	Split text into multiple columns	=SUBSTITUTE("Hello, old world","old","new")
45	=INDEX(Sheet2!A2:A100,SMALL(IF(Sheet2!B2:B100="Category1",ROW(Sheet2!A2:A100)-ROW(Sheet2!A2)+1),ROW(1:1)))	Replace text in a cell with new text	=INDEX(Sheet2!A2:A100,SMALL(IF(Sheet2!B2:B100="Category1",ROW(Sheet2!A2:A100)-ROW(Sheet2!A2)+1),ROW(1:1)))
46	=CONCATENATE(TEXT(A2,"yyyy")," - ",TEXT(B2,"mmm"))	Extract multiple matching values	=CONCATENATE(TEXT(A2,"yyyy")," - ",TEXT(B2,"mmm"))

47	=IFERROR(VLOOKUP(A2,Sheet2!A2:B100,2,FALSE),"Not Found")	Combine date and month into text	=IFERROR(VLOOKUP("ValueX",Sheet2!A2:B100,2,FALSE),"Not Found")
48	=IFERROR(INDEX(Sheet2!B2:B100,MATCH(A2,Sheet2!A2:A100,0)),"No Match")	Handle errors in VLOOKUP with custom text	=IFERROR(INDEX(Sheet2!B2:B100,MATCH("ValueX",Sheet2!A2:A100,0)),"No Match")
49	=SUMPRODUCT(--(TEXT(A2:A100,"mmm")="Mar"),C2:C100)	Handle errors in INDEX-MATCH with custom text	=SUMPRODUCT(--(TEXT(A2:A100,"mmm")="Mar"),C2:C100)

CONCLUSION

The updated Excel models have all you need to get started and become a professional, as well as a wide range of valuable features. To save you time, MS Excel identifies trends and organizes results. Create spreadsheets quickly and conveniently from models or from scratch, then use modern features to conduct calculations.

It includes both basic and advanced software that can be used in almost any business environment. The Excel database helps you build, access, update, and exchange data with others efficiently and easily. You can generate spreadsheets, data tables, data logs, budgets, and more by reading and updating excel files attached to emails.

When you gain a better understanding of various definitions, you'll be able to recognize the new tools and features that Excel offers its users. The reality is that Excel functionality can accommodate almost any individual or business needs. All you need to do is put in the effort to broaden your skills. The learning curve for developing your skills may be steep, but with practice and time, you will notice that things become second nature. After all, a person improves by repetition.

Mastering these basic Excel skills is what you need to do to make your life easier—and maybe impress those in your workplace. However, remember that no matter how familiar you are with this helpful instrument, there is always something fresh to learn.

Whatever you do, keep developing your Excel skills—it will not only help you keep track of your own earnings, but it can also lead to a better potential job opportunity.

To conclude, wisdom is often said to be strong, and there's no easier way to motivate yourself than by honing your talents and the worth of your business with expertise and technology.

Made in the USA
Las Vegas, NV
14 June 2024